D1106809

Financing
Higher Education

THE LIBRARY OF EDUCATION

A Project of The Center for Applied Research in Education, Inc.

G. R. Gottschalk, Director

Categories of Coverage

I	II	III
Curriculum and Teaching	Administration, Organization, and Finance	Psychology

IV	V	VI
History, Philosophy, and Social Foundations	Professional Skills	Educational Institutions

Financing Higher Education

M. M. CHAMBERS

Visiting Professor of Higher Education
The University of Michigan

1963
The Center for Applied Research in Education, Inc.
Washington, D.C.

Library of Congress
Catalog Card No.: 63–17319

PRINTED IN THE UNITED STATES OF AMERICA

Foreword

Education beyond the high school bids fair to become, by about 1970, an enterprise involving annual receipts and expenditures of $10 billion to $12 billion. Although this will probably be less than 2 per cent of the gross national product, this percentage will be substantially higher than it has ever been. Higher education is now and will continue to be an increasingly crucial element in the national and individual lives of the American people.

This book is addressed to a wider audience than those persons engaged in university or college business management, or fund raising, or general administration. It is an effort to disclose, in forthright words and with uncluttered expression, some of the elementary facts about where colleges and universities get their income, how they spend it, and what some of the more obvious trends in the larger aspects of these matters appear to be. It discusses some of the issues which are currently controversial, with a modicum of historical allusions to afford a background.

The viewpoint is not primarily that of the individual student or his family seeking to surmount their private financial stress, although this problem receives some brief attention in the final chapter. Rather it is that of the intelligent citizen—of whatever age, sex, or status—who wants to think about the roles that higher education will probably play in the economy of the nation during the ensuing years; who senses the growing impact of learning in the twentieth century world, and wishes to comprehend the ways and means of providing for its support, and to participate in the forming of public policies concerning it.

ALGO D. HENDERSON
Director, Center for the Study of Higher Education
The University of Michigan

Contents

CHAPTER I

The Background of College Financial Support 1

Trends Affecting Costs and Income 1
The Great Depression of the 1930's 5
The Two World Wars 7
Some Changes of the Post-War Period 10
Summarizing Some Tendencies 15

CHAPTER II

Where the Money Comes From: Income from Nontax Sources 18

Private Donors as Sources of Income 19
Student Fees 27
Endowment as a Source of Income 29

CHAPTER III

Where the Money Comes From: Income from Tax Sources 31

The Complicated Backdrop of the Revenue System 32
Support from Local Taxing Units 33
Support from the States 38
The Federal Government's Participation 50

CHAPTER IV

Issues Regarding the Sources of Support 58

The Future of Private Philanthropy 59
High Fees or Public Support? 60
The Rationale of Student Aids 64
The Trend Toward Public Support 69

CHAPTER V

Where the Money Goes: Some Categories of Current Expenditure 71

Auxiliary Enterprises and Student Aid 72
Educational and General Activities Other Than Instruction and Research 73
Faculty Pay: Nonacademic Salaries and Wages 76

CHAPTER VI

Efficiency in Higher Education 84

Unit Costs of Instruction 85
Utilization of Plant Facilities 91
Efficient Management of Investments 92
Formulas as Guides in the Allocation of Funds to Groups of Similar Institutions 93
The Future of Formulas 97

CHAPTER VII

The Sources of Real Waste and Loss 102

A Mainspring of the National Economy 103
Failure to Develop Talents Is the Nation's Loss 103

Comparisons Among States 104
International Comparisons 105
Failure to Develop Talents Is the Individual's Loss Also 106
Advice to Today's Students and Their Families 107

Bibliography 111

Index 113

CHAPTER I

The Background of College Financial Support

Colleges and universities, in common with other organizations and individuals in society, must constantly buy many types of goods and services essential to their operation. If an institution offers living accommodations, it is "selling" lodgings and meals and laundry services to its students. If it charges fees for tuition, it is "selling" the services of its teachers and the use of its instructional facilities. Often colleges sell some surplus products of their laboratories, shops, and farms. (These endeavors are not emphasized lest private vendors of the same commodities complain about "unfair" competition.)

Hundreds of additional specific examples could be cited to illustrate that a college buys and, to a limited extent, sells an amazing variety of goods and services. Thus a college is subject to short- and long-term fluctuations in prices and interest rates and to other aspects of the business cycle. It is also affected by long-range economic trends.

Trends Affecting Costs and Income

Such phenomena will be considered as the shift from an agricultural to an industrial economy, the increase of productivity of manpower in both agriculture and industry, the growth of population and other social changes which increase the labor supply, and the impact of advancing technology upon ways of living and habits of consumption and spending.

Within the same range are trends such as the long, slow movement toward "socialization" of the economy, so that perhaps a third or more of the total volume of all transactions involves the national, state, or local government; and so that the total "bite" of taxation at all levels embraces a really substantial portion of the aggregate of all private incomes.

The price curve. For many decades the trend of prices has been generally upward, though with many and violent fluctuations. What are the effects of this long-continued inflationary trend?

Perhaps the principal effect is that the buying power of wages, salaries, retirement allowances, and other fixed incomes declines. Thus the college finds that its faculty members and other employees are demanding higher pay, not only in the form of normal increments, but also because the pay schedules adopted in previous years have become grossly inadequate because of rising prices.

A mercantile business can turn a profit by selling goods purchased last year at lower prices; but a college is not in that business, and so rising prices merely mean that this year's supplies will cost more than last year's. Rising prices simply mean rising costs of operation, and a college has no way of offsetting them except by charging more for meals and lodgings, and perhaps by raising its fees for tuition and other services. These are only partial offsets, and the necessity of increasing income from gifts or public appropriations or both continues.

Student fees have more than doubled in the past two decades, but even now students in public institutions pay only an average of about 18 per cent of the educational and general operating costs, while students in private institutions pay about 55 per cent. In only rare instances do students pay the full costs and, as one college president has pointed out, any extension of such a plan is practically unthinkable for numerous reasons. For one thing, the donors of endowment funds to colleges and universities over the past three hundred years have made their donations in order to provide education at less than cost. This purpose is undoubtedly the essence of their intent and a tacit condition of their gifts, so that departure from it would constitute a breach of trust.[1]

Many other grave disadvantages would attend a policy of increasing fees. Such a policy is not an approved answer to the pinch of rising prices.

Fluctuations in interest rates. When interest rates go down, the income from invested endowment funds is not as high as before. At the same time, a drop in interest rates has an inflationary tendency, with a likelihood of causing rises in the prices of goods and services.

---

[1] Robert P. Ludlum, "How High Should Tuition Go?" *Educational Record,* 39 (October, 1958), 306–10.

Therefore it has a nutcracker effect upon endowed colleges. Some forms of investment, however, tend to counteract this effect. Land and real property in general, as well as common stocks, tend to increase in value and to provide increasing income in times of rising prices. The income from good common stocks is more responsive to changes in the business cycle, in general, than the income from real estate. These are some of the reasons why endowment investments are diversified, and why during the past thirty years there has been a substantial increase in the proportions that common stocks occupy in college and university investment portfolios.[2]

In recent decades the Federal Reserve Board, an agency of the national government, has possessed the power to influence interest rates through regulations governing the operation of national banks (mainly by changing the discount rate or rate of interest at which Federal Reserve Banks make loans to member banks). In some recent instances it has cautiously exercised these powers, so that in the 1950's interest rates rose slightly. A tightening of the money market is a deflationary measure—or perhaps it is better described as a counterinflationary tactic; and the powers placed in the hands of the Federal Reserve Board constitute one device among many designed to put the fluctuations of the business cycle under some form of restraint. One theory is that prices and wages should be allowed to rise no faster than the rate at which industrial productivity increases.

The declining role of endowment. The growth of enrollments and the rise in costs have been so rapid that they have compelled colleges to rely on current gifts and appropriations and student fees as principal sources of income. Income from endowment income constitutes only 14 per cent of the total incomes of private institutions, and only 2 per cent of the income of the public establishments. It is well to be aware, too, that endowments are of slight importance except in relatively few institutions. Of all the nearly 2000 institutions in the United States, only 75 have endowments of $10 million or more, and of these only 16 have permanent funds of over $50 million. Millett makes the statement that in 1950 only eighteen out of 57 private universities had endowment income of $1 million or

---

[2] For example, 60 per cent of Princeton's $140 million endowment in 1958 was invested in selected common stocks.

more, and that these eighteen received 87 per cent of the endowment income of all universities.[3]

Prior to about 1930 the large philanthropic foundations often made grants to colleges for endowment, and it was generally believed that under ideal conditions an institution might get as much as half of its total income from endowment. If this situation were to be brought about now for all institutions, it would require $20 billion in endowment funds, or seven times the present aggregrate of endowments. Since 1930 the foundations have not stressed gifts of permanent funds (a major exception being the Ford Foundation grants of $.5 billion in 1956 for endowment of faculty salaries). Colleges have learned that recurrent gifts for current expenses, coming from annual campaigns (among church members, alumni, "friends," business corporations, the local community, and philanthropic donors) can, if developed and cultivated, become as dependable a source of income as endowment itself. This is what fund-raisers mean when they speak of "living endowment."

Another factor is the decline of the untrammeled opportunity to build vast private fortunes which characterized the nineteenth and early twentieth centuries. Since 1930 the more and more steeply graduated income tax rates, plus estate and inheritance taxes and other influences, have greatly reduced the likelihood of huge personal accumulations equal to those of the private philanthropists who were bequeathing their fortunes to endowment funds in the early part of this century.

Again, there is a theory held by some economists and other social scientists that the freezing of liquid wealth in large endowments is socially undesirable because it removes these funds from the venturesome field of risk investments in untried enterprises. There are still others who believe it effects too great a concentration of power in the hands of the managers of large endowments: they point to the alleged tendency of perpetual charitable trusts to become conservative or reactionary in their management—or even to deteriorate to a point where they have no social utility at all—when bound by the terms of a trust instrument originally designed to meet needs which have now disappeared or to advance purposes which have long since been fully achieved.

---

[3] John D. Millett, *Financing Higher Education in the United States* (New York: Columbia University Press, 1952), p. 308.

Despite all that has been said about the decline of endowments in relative importance, as well as the theoretical objections to them, endowments are still growing at a moderate pace and the donor's freedom of choice to contribute to endowment is as wide as it ever was. Indeed, equity jurisprudence in the American states is now in general more favorable toward sustaining the validity and fostering the execution of charitable gifts and bequests than it was a half-century ago.

The Great Depression of the 1930's

The biggest punctuation mark in the economic trends of the past half-century is the financial depression of the early 1930's. From the viewpoint of college finance, its effects can be conveniently classified in two groups: (1) immediate effects upon college business management, financial support, college attendance, and related matters; and (2) long-range effects resulting from the new legislation and permanent economic changes which followed. A third outcome of great significance might be attributed to it: the marked slowing down of the birth rate during the 1930's.

When the stringency threatened to compel thousands of students to withdraw because of lack of financial means, a relief measure in the form of limited payments of federal money for work, assigned and supervised by the college authorities, was put into operation. During 1933–35 this operation was administered by the Federal Emergency Relief Administration, after which it became one of the two principal responsibilities of the National Youth Administration. Such of these agencies as had not already passed into limbo were abolished in the prelude to World War II, when unemployment and destitution were supplanted by compulsory military service and employment in war industries at high wages.

But these measures provided the knowledge that if a disaster of the magnitude of the panic of 1932 ever occurs again, it will be possible to prevent decimation of the colleges by reviving some such measure as the Student Work Program of the National Youth Administration. A contemporary and better-publicized organization was the Civilian Conservation Corps, through which hundreds of thousands of out-of-school boys were taken off city streets and put into well-fed and well-disciplined units in work camps on public and private lands. There they performed conservation work and received wages and some instruction, and usually went home stronger and more competent than before.

The history of the period gives rise to some reflections and questions as to what might be the role of the colleges if a similar emergency should occur again. How might the measures of 1933–40 be modified and improved? What were their strengths and weaknesses? Should any of their elements become permanent, rather than mere emergency expedients? Did the colleges suffer any harm from their transitory liaison with the federal government? Here is material for a dissertation on a phase of the history of higher education.

Another effect of the stringency in the early 1930's was the halting of building operations on the campus. The situation was ameliorated somewhat by occasional loans from the Reconstruction Finance Corporation and by a program of loans and grants from the Public Works Administration. These set in motion a more or less intermittent chain of federal measures which have continued down to the present. A tracing of the fortunes of these measures and their outcomes is also worthy of much study for they, too, raise questions which are as timely today as they were in 1935. What role should the federal government take in the provision of physical plant facilities for colleges and universities?

Some long-run effects. The 1930's marked a pervasive revolution in the social and economic scene, and the end of an era. Legislation, in one major act after another, revamped the relationship between the federal government and business, created built-in cushions against a recurrence of financial panic, and set up schemes of social security on such a scale that they will not come into full normal operation until a half-century after their enactment. The volume of federal expenditures was put upon an unprecedentedly high level (soon to be dwarfed, to be sure, by war and "cold" war outlays), and federal taxes, especially the income tax, were pushed upward while increased borrowings raised the federal debt to astronomic proportions.

This revolution of the 1930's has subtly altered many aspects of the modern economic cosmos. It gave rise to an emphasis upon human rights as against property rights, which in turn produced a permanent narrowing of the spread among economic classes. The magnification of the role of organized labor helped to usher in an era in which the average truck driver earns as much as an assistant professor of philosophy in an accredited college. This may mean that the truck driver's children may be able to go to college, and may help to explain why the proportion of college-age persons actually attending college continually rises. This tendency was reversed neither by World War II nor by the postwar period, both of which brought unexampled prosperity and continued (but fortunately somewhat gradual) inflation.

The Two World Wars

During World War I, the War Department—already beginning to appreciate the value of college training as an element of military strength—soon put into effect a scheme whereby the physically fit male population of the colleges could continue their studies while receiving much the same military training as their confrères were receiving in army camps. The necessary cadres of officers and non-commissioned officers were detailed to each campus participating in the program, and arms and equipment were supplied. Physically fit students were enlisted, uniformed, and put under the discipline of the Articles of War, at the same time undergoing a stiff schedule of military training with allowance for the continuation of at least part of their college studies. The organization, known as the Students' Army Training Corps, was not in full operation until October 1918, only a few weeks before the suspension of hostilities on November 11. Naturally it brought a very great disruption and dislocation of the accustomed routine in the colleges and was generally deplored and resented by presidents and faculties, especially because in the haste of wartime the army personnel detailed for training duty were often not qualified for work in a college community. Because the program was of short duration, there was no real test of its efficacy as a method of utilizing colleges and college students in wartime.

Peacetime conscription was enacted by Congress more than a year before Pearl Harbor, and since that time the devising of suitable regulations regarding deferment of college students has been one of the foremost problems of the Selective Service System. Many times it has been necessary to modify the rules to fit changed circumstances; but in general the policy of keeping good students (especially those in science and engineering fields) in college until maximum benefit has been achieved has been adhered to.[4] This involves placing upon such students an obligation to a period of military service after leaving college. More or less close adherence to this policy had much to do with preventing the decimation of male student bodies. Only in one war year (1943–44) was there a very heavy drop in college enrollments. This was occasioned largely by the departure of young men for military service, but partly by the employment of young women in war industries.

For the hundreds of privately controlled colleges which depend upon student fees for half or more than half of their annual income, this drop in enrollment might have been catastrophic, but the blow was somewhat softened by the fact that many younger male faculty members were going into the armed services either voluntarily or by conscription, while others of all ages and both sexes were accepting jobs as civilian employees in the war-swollen governmental agencies or in industry. Thus the colleges were able to reduce their operating expenses considerably to approach conformity with the decline in enrollments.

The colleges in the service of the nation. During World War II the Navy utilized a considerable number of colleges as officer-training stations, enrolling qualified students in training units under military discipline but permitting them to complete their studies. The largest of these programs was designated "V-12" (for deck and engineering officers). Rather late in the war the Army instituted its Army Specialized Training Program (ASTP), under which selected students were enlisted and placed in uniform but allowed to continue their studies for varying periods, depending upon the Army's needs for specialists. The specialties most in demand were in technology and modern languages, but one phase of this program was organized especially for students of medicine and dentistry. The Army Air Forces recruited flying cadets direct from civilian life, and many of them were college students. Aside from the flying training stations for air cadets, both the Army and the Air Forces departed from the World War I practice of conducting officers' training camps for selected recruits direct from civilian life. Instead they used the Officer Candidate School (OCS) system, under which the short and intensive all-military officer-candidate schools were open only

[4] M. H. Trytten, *Student Deferment in Selective Service: A Vital Factor in National Security* (Minneapolis: University of Minnesota Press, 1952).

to selected enlisted men who had proved themselves to be good soldiers by several months of enlisted service, and whose scores on the Army General Classification Test were not less than 110.

It should be added that both the Army and the Navy continued their Reserve Officers' Training Corps (ROTC) units in colleges and universities throughout the war, though on somewhat abbreviated and accelerated schedules. The ROTC programs had been conducted continuously since 1920, and had produced a great many of the older reserve officers who were called to active duty in World War II, as well as the younger ones who were turned out during the war.

Among the outcomes of the war experience for the colleges a few may be easily enumerated:

1. There was a distinct and widespread recognition of higher education as an instrument of national policy and as an element in national defense.
2. Considerable experience was gained in the negotiation of compensation by the government to the colleges for the use of their facilities and personnel in war training programs.[5]
3. Various governmental measures prevented the war from bringing financial disaster to many private colleges and prevented the whole higher educational enterprise from being greatly weakened or partly suspended during the war period.
4. The inflation which traditionally accompanies all wars was to a considerable extent held in check by governmental price controls, rent controls, and related measures. As it was, the limited inflation increased the financial difficulties of the colleges; but without governmental controls, unlimited inflation would have probably ruined many of them. Their difficulties were increased by the removal of price controls in 1946, but this time they were saved by the huge influx of government-subsidized veterans as students.

Another result of World War II which has bearing upon college financing was the pressure built up during the war for "acceleration" of college courses. In wartime the military academies adopt an accelerated program and turn out young officers a year or more ahead of schedule. All the vast congeries of schools conducted by and within the armed services for their own personnel were operated on

---

[5] Raymond J. Connolly, "Financial Aspects of the College Training Programs," in *College Training Programs of the Armed Services,* by H. C. Herge, *et al.* (Washington, D.C.: American Council on Education, 1948), pp. 133–77.

an intensive, "hurry-up" basis. The schools were set up for a particular purpose, usually narrowly and explicitly defined, and for their purposes they were successful in marked degree. Young lawyers and Latin teachers who had never had a wrench in their hands became airplane mechanics in six weeks. Astonishingly good results were obtained from short and extremely intensive courses in modern foreign languages, including the exotic tongues of Africa and the Orient. Thus there was an impulse toward revolutionizing college curriculums and teaching methods, at least in their quantitative aspects, in the hope that what had traditionally been accomplished in four years might well be done in two and a half or three.

This suggestion was smolderingly resisted by a majority of faculty members, many of whom argued that higher education should really never be ad hoc, and that learning and a leisurely pace are inseparable. On the other hand, some distinguished psychologists and educators (such as Sidney L. Pressey of Ohio State University) made studies of the subject and published reports indicating that the idea of acceleration was by no means wholly without merit.[6]

Some Changes of the Post-War Period

Studies of acceleration were doomed to be largely ignored, however, in the euphoric feeling of release that came with the end of the long war; they were lost in the huge administrative confusion that was caused by the necessity of making room for the influx of veterans, many of whom brought wives and babies with them, and wrought another permanent change in campus life.

Although the thought of acceleration was widely sneered at and largely ignored, few mature persons familiar with college life will deny that the campus today has a much more businesslike air than prevailed before the war. Adult veterans bearing family responsibilities and seeking to prepare as rapidly as possible for a remunerative occupation did not behave like eighteen-year-olds fresh from high school. They were not happy at arriving in a classroom and finding a scrawl on the blackboard announcing "Professor X will not meet his class today." They expected to find Professor X, or at least his substitute, and to get ahead with the day's work. They did not insist

[6] Sidney L. Pressey, "Acceleration: Perspectives, Appraisals, Implications," in *College Training Programs of the Armed Services, op. cit.*, pp. 85–103.

on having their mornings free for sleep, their afternoons free for golf, or their evenings free for bull-sessions.

There are now more afternoon and evening classes, longer library hours, and less class-cutting, drinking, and general dilly-dallying than in the good old days. The professor who once ambled about under the elms in a pipe-smoking daze is now more apt to meet his appointments punctually, speak crisply and to the point, and keep himself aware of the legitimate needs of many types of students. For example, if a student commutes forty miles to a class which ends at 6 P.M. and wants a private conference immediately after class, he gets it, though it means a long day and a delayed dinner to professor and student alike.

Matters of this kind do not enter into the institutional accounting system; nevertheless, they mark an unmistakable change in the atmosphere of the campus. Also it is quite obvious that a high percentage of faculty members today are aware of their responsibilities to the public as well. Many of them, in addition to carrying full teaching loads, conduct research, provide consultative services when called upon, and participate in the leadership of public and private nonprofit agencies. These activities, useful in their own right, enrich and improve their teaching. All this is a far cry from the secluded and leisurely life within the ivied walls of old.

The cold war. Everyone expected at least a temporary economic decline after World War II. The rapid demobilization of seven or eight million members of the armed services was expected to give rise to widespread unemployment. At the same time great industrial plants had to be reconverted from the manufacture of war materials to the making of automobiles, washing machines, refrigerators, and myriad peacetime gadgets.

The late great Senator Robert A. Taft, insisting upon the abolition of price controls in 1946, predicted that price levels would immediately drop from their wartime heights. Instead, the price levels spurted upward and the inflationary trend has been practically continuous for a decade and a half, with only occasional slight and short-lived recessions.

This long inflationary trend has been sustained in part by the most gigantic governmental expenditures in history, particularly during the decade of the 1950's. These expenditures were occasioned by the long-drawn-out and apparently nonameliorable phase of dark suspicion, mutual fear, and distrust between the government of the United States and that of the Soviet Union.

Thus it has come about that the total federal budget for recent fiscal years has been of the order of $80 billion, about half of which is allotted for defense. Another block of some $8 billion goes as military and technical aid to various countries in all parts of the world, principally for the purpose of bolstering their military strength but also for improving living conditions for their underprivileged peoples.

Still another block of some $8 billion must now go for interest on the national debt of some $300 billion. An interesting footnote is that the recent rise in interest rates has nearly doubled the amount required for servicing the debt within the past five years.

It is clear that only a minor fraction of the federal budget is going for the domestic functions of the federal government. The total annual expenditure is so huge that, despite the fact that there is usually a comparatively small annual deficit, the revenues collected annually by the federal government aggregate more than twice the taxes collected by the states and local subdivisions combined. The changing relationships among annual revenues collected by the three levels of government in the revenue picture are indicated in Table 1.

TABLE 1

FEDERAL, STATE, AND LOCAL TAX REVENUES SINCE 1940 (IN MILLIONS) *

Year (1)	*Federal* (2)	*State* (3)	*Local* (4)
1940	5,340	4,171	4,606
1950	35,053	7,930	7,984
1957	69,815	14,531	14,511

* Derived from the *Statistical Abstract of the United States*. This table is adapted from Maynard Bemis, "Men and Money," *Phi Delta Kappan,* 40 (March, 1959), 240–42.

This trend toward diverting a major part of our total disposable public funds to nonconstructive purposes, necessary though it may be, is a massive obstacle to the progress of civilization in our time. If only 5 per cent of the current year's expenditures for defense could be transferred to higher education, the national total of expenditures for higher education would be nearly doubled. A saving element is the fact that small parts of the huge defense expenditures are used for scientific research and development, a minor portion of which is carried on under contract with universities.

From the long-run viewpoint of national survival, it will be well to keep an eye on the indices of industrial production from year to year and from decade to decade in such parts of the world as the Soviet Union and the People's Republic of China. At present these indices are moving upward swiftly while production in the United States is advancing at only a negligible rate. If this country is to retain its world leadership, it will eventually have to encourage education beyond the high school to develop on an unprecedented scale and to achieve heights of excellence never before attained. It is not too soon to recognize this.

Population trends. Most students of population believe that the marked slowdown in the birth rate which characterized the 1930's was caused by the economic depression. There is, of course, no conclusive proof. Suffice it to say that the leading experts of that day, including those in the U.S. Census Bureau, the U.S. Public Health Service, the Scripps Institute of Population Studies, and various universities, showed that if the trends were projected without change the population of the United States would level off at about 130 million at about the year 1944, and that there might be no great increases or decreases for some time thereafter.[7]

As everyone knows now, the war period 1940–46 brought a baby boom of unprecedented proportions so that the annual number of births climbed from the accustomed two million to nearer four million, with the most profound and pervasive consequences for the future. For example, babies born in 1941 were of college-entrance age in 1959. Such increases in college enrollment as had occurred in previous years occurred despite the almost level birth curve of the 1930's; from now on they will be jet-assisted by the zooming birth curve of the 1940's. Another sidelight: the babies of 1941 and subsequent years are now entering the normal age of parenthood; since they will be much more numerous than any previous similar age group, there may well be a renewed baby boom in the 1960's unless

[7] See the population chapter in *How Fare American Youth?* A Report to the American Youth Commission (Washington, D.C.: American Council on Education, 1938).

some variable factor causes a decline in the birth rate per 1000 women of childbearing age.

Consider one more element. During the "veterans' bulge" of 1946–50, many babies were born while their parents, or at least their fathers, were college students. These parents will want their children to go to college. By about 1964–68, the children who were born on the campus will be returning to it, along with many of their brothers and sisters.

As has been amply demonstrated, future birth rates cannot be predicted with much confidence; but it is possible to estimate the college-age population for some eighteen to twenty-one years in advance with very great likelihood of accuracy, because the persons involved are already born. It is only necessary to make suitable allowances for such factors as deaths, disabilities, in-migration, and out-migration. Thus it is known that the college-age population in 1970–75 will be about twice what it was in 1960.

The actual college enrollment is a little more difficult to forecast, for it depends upon the proportion of persons of college age who actually attend; or, more accurately, the proportion that the total college enrollment bears to the total population of college age. This proportion has risen from 4 per cent in 1900 to about 31 per cent in 1958; and this does not augur any decline between 1960 and 1970 or beyond. It is conceivable, indeed, that at some point a distinct flattening-out of the curve may take place, but this may not occur until the percentage reaches 50 or higher.

The upgrading of all occupations. A powerful factor that will keep the trend upward is the upgrading of all occupations that accompanies advances in technology, so that there is constant need not only for more top-level scientists and professional people, but also for a vast array of persons of only relatively less competence to fill the rapidly increasing number of semiprofessional and subprofessional jobs.

This tremendously important trend is shown in part by the figures in Table 2.

One of the principal shortcomings of these figures is that they do not show the change in the character of farming as an occupation. Whereas in 1900 most farmers and farm workers were manual laborers with few and simple technical skills, today farming has become much more largely a large-scale technical and managerial occupation.

TABLE 2

PERCENTAGES OF ALL GAINFUL WORKERS OCCUPIED IN THREE PRINCIPAL OCCUPATIONAL GROUPS SINCE 1900, WITH PROJECTIONS TO 1975 *

Year	*Professional and Technical*	*Farm* **	*Laborers (Industrial)*
(1)	(2)	(3)	(4)
1900	4.4	37.5	12.5
1920	5.4	27.0	11.6
1940	7.5	17.4	9.4
1950	8.6	11.8	6.6
1965	11.3	7.6	5.5
1975	14.0	5.3	4.4

* Adapted from *Citizens Speak Out on School Costs* (Washington, D.C.: National Education Association, 1959), p. 13.
** Includes owners, managers, and laborers.

The doubling of college enrollments by 1970 or thereabouts is accepted by even the most conservative of social scientists. What does this mean to the financing of higher education? Seymour E. Harris, professor of economics at Harvard University, says the total annual outlay for the operating expenses of higher education will rise from about $3 billion in 1958 to at least $9 billion ten to twelve years later: He justifies this prediction in an awkward but eloquent sentence:

> Never have we had to contend with such a change in the proportion of those of college age, with so unusual a rise of interest in going to college, associated in turn with a rise of income levels that makes it possible increasingly to go to college, with an improvement in financing methods and a rise in the proportion of young people able to go to college within commuting distance, and hence at savings in expenses.[8]

Summarizing Some Tendencies

We have suggested that economic and social trends, as well as the slowly changing traditions of college and university life and of the academic profession, influence college financial management in

[8] Seymour E. Harris, "College Salaries, Financing of Higher Education, and Management of Institutions of Higher Learning," *Bulletin of the American Association of University Professors,* 44 (Summer, 1958), 589–95.

ways that are many and profound. All these trends can be traced in the past; some are more difficult to forecast in the future than others. For example, it is far more difficult to predict what the birth rate will be five years in the future than it is to predict what the number of persons of college age will be fifteen years from now—and to predict the advent of war or depression is rather more hazardous than either. But out of the general uncertainty certain major tendencies emerge as almost inevitable. In connection with these, however, questions of policy intrude—questions which must be considered, debated, and settled by compromise, by agreement, or by the logic of events.

1. Aside from the fact that the population of college age is due to increase rapidly, the proportion of those persons wanting to attend college seems sure to increase also. Should the policy be to encourage and foster the fulfillment of that desire? Or to set limits which would discourage and defeat that ambition except for a limited number of the more fortunate?

2. Depression, war, and cold war have made higher education increasingly a matter of national concern. Visible economic changes make it practically certain that this tendency will continue. Higher education has become an instrument of national policy. Does this mean that the freedom and diversity of American colleges and universities must be diminished? If higher education is in a paramount sense a means of strengthening the national manpower resources, what bearing has this upon the question of how large the college enrollment should be?

3. The numerous trends pointing toward both a relative and absolute increase in college costs indicate that institutions of all types must augment their incomes. Gifts from private sources are growing, but not at a sufficient rate to make a major impression. Endowment income is coming to be of minor importance. Student fees have, on average, more than doubled in the past twenty years; but there are compelling reasons which make it highly unlikely that they can be made to approach full payment of educational costs, even in private institutions. In public institutions they must continue at modest levels, or perhaps be abolished altogether, to keep open the gates of opportunity to the capable, and to continue the great traditions of the state universities and the land-grant colleges. These factors make two conclusions seem inescapable: (a) support from

public funds must grow at a rapid rate; (b) the proportion of the total student enrollment going into public institutions of all types, including community colleges, will increase. Though there are many indications that the private institutions will maintain their strength and grow somewhat, the public institutions must grow even more rapidly.

The situation will afford further opportunity to refine the differences in institutional programs and to add to the diversity of the opportunities offered in a statewide system and in the national panorama. Private institutions can and will continue to play an indispensable role, quantitatively somewhat larger than at present, but relatively considerably smaller. Private support will continue and grow, but relatively greater growth must take place in support from public sources. This is already a major trend in the financing of higher education.

CHAPTER II

Where the Money Comes From: Income from Nontax Sources

Colleges and universities derive income from a few main sources: (1) private donors, (2) endowment funds, (3) governmental units, (4) students, and (5) miscellaneous activities such as sales of products and the operation of auxiliary enterprises.

Public and private institutions differ rather markedly as to their reliance on these sources. For privately controlled colleges and universities the largest item is usually student fees; income from governmental units is usually negligible. Gifts from private donors are also comparatively important to these institutions and, for a few of the wealthier ones, income from endowment is large.

On the other hand, colleges and universities under public control generally find that appropriations of tax money from national, state, or local governments are their major sustenance. Student fees play a much lesser role. Some have endowment funds and practically all receive private gifts, but these are not relatively so important to them, though they are increasing in amount.

The situation is illustrated in Table 3, which shows the principal sources of income for private and public universities and colleges as of a recent year.

TABLE 3

SOURCES OF INCOME OF INSTITUTIONS OF HIGHER EDUCATION, 1955 *

Income (1)	*Private* (2)	*Public* (3)
Students fees	55%	18%
Endowment Income	14	2
Gifts	19	3
Governments	4	72
Other sources	8	5
	100	100

* From *The Closing College Door* (New York: Council for Financial Aid to Education, Inc.).

Private Donors as Sources of Income

The idea of education as an object of private charity is ancient. In modern times the charter of an educational institution always authorizes it to receive gifts to be used for its educational purposes. Many individuals, philanthropic organizations, business corporations, and other associations are inclined for various reasons to give money or property for education. Harvard derives its name from the man who bequeathed his library to it soon after its founding. It is said that when twelve clergymen met for the first conference which led to the establishment of Yale, each brought a book to be donated to the college. Private contributions may come to a college through gifts, bequests, contracts of subscription, or other channels; and delivery or payment may be immediate or deferred.

A gift is said to be general or unrestricted if the donor does not specify any purpose for which it must be used, other than the general educational purposes of the institution. It is said to be restricted if it carries a stipulation that it shall be used for a particular purpose, such as for the erection or maintenance of a particular building, faculty salaries, a particular department of instruction, scholarships, or a stained-glass window in the college chapel.

Unrestricted gifts are much to be preferred, for they can be used for any purpose deemed most needful by the college administration, and their acceptance does not involve any enforced modification or distortion of the plans or policies of the institution.

Some types of restricted gifts work very well. For example, alumni are often solicited for contributions to be used to improve faculty salaries, and their affection for their former professors—coupled with their knowledge that academic pay is grossly inadequate—often leads them to respond well. Often a state university solicits gifts for relatively rare and risky research projects for which legislatures are reluctant to provide tax funds. Private givers who know something of the vast potential of the projects may be willing to take the gamble and contribute as a form of public service.

The types of restricted gifts are innumerable, and sometimes the strings attached may make the gift a detriment rather than a benefit to the institution. For example, a gift of an ornate building unaccompanied by any endowment for its operation and maintenance saddles the institution with the continuing expenses of heating, lighting, cleaning, preservation, and repair—and these may be burdensome if the building is not of a type to fit well into the layout of the campus and to meet a need of the college program. To look a gift horse in the mouth may seem ungrateful, but in fact prudence sometimes impels a college to reject an offer of a restricted gift which would become a "white elephant."

Gifts may be for endowment (permanent funds held in trust, with only their income to be expended), for capital outlay (land, buildings, equipment), or for current expenses (salaries and wages, supplies, or other items necessary in operating the institution).

The total of private gifts to institutions of higher education is currently well above $1 billion per year. The Council for Financial Aid to Education has reported that 1032 colleges and universities received an aggregate of $803 million from these sources during the year 1960–61. The relative contributions of six categories of givers are shown in Table 4.

TABLE 4

SIX CATEGORIES OF PRIVATE CONTRIBUTORS TO 1032 COLLEGES AND UNIVERSITIES 1960–61, AND THEIR APPROXIMATE AGGREGATE CONTRIBUTIONS (IN MILLIONS)

(1)	(2)
Philanthropic Foundations	$195.5
Nonalumni Individuals	180.3
Alumni	174.9
Business Corporations	131.1
Religious Denominations	73.5
Other Sources	47.8
Total	803.1

Source: "Voluntary Support of America's Colleges and Universities," *The New York Times* (July 8, 1962).

Apparently about 83 per cent of all these private gifts went to privately controlled institutions, and a little over 16 per cent to state and municipal universities. The rates of increase over the preceding six-year period (since 1954–55) from all the categories has been rapid, being reported as ranging from 76 per cent to 289 per cent.

Philanthropic foundations. Higher education is not the exclusive object of the bounty of the great "general purpose" or "benefit of mankind" foundations, but it is often a favorite one. A total of some 600 foundations are listed in Rich's *American Foundations and Their Fields.*[1] During the past half-century at least 110 of these foundations have accumulated assets of more than $10 million each. Among the better known and larger ones are the Carnegie, Commonwealth, Ford, Guggenheim, Hayden, Kellogg, Lilly, Mellon, Rockefeller, Sloan, and Twentieth Century.

There is no doubt that the impact of foundation giving has much more pervasive effects upon the development of higher education than its current total flow of some $200 million a year would indicate. For one thing foundation grants are sometimes made on the condition they be "matched" by funds obtained from other sources. At various times the prevailing emphasis has seemed to shift somewhat from gifts for endowment to gifts for capital outlay to grants for research. Interspersed have been some significant outlays specifically aimed at improving faculty salaries and fringe benefits.

Most foundation directors and officers have an eye on maximizing the outcomes of their programs by supporting salutary educational innovations and experimentation which could hardly be initiated without philanthropic aid, but which, if adjudged successful, will eventually find their way into general practice. Some foundations have pursued a policy, at least in part, of building up peaks of excellence by concentrating upon grants to what were deemed to be the institutions or departments of highest quality.

For the most part the record of the foundations in distributing grants where they will do the most good seems to be excellent (though of course some errors are inevitable), but they have been criticized for a policy of too often allotting research grants for minutely planned projects rather than making them available without strings to individual scholars or researchers of recognized potential. Probably this emphasis is shifting somewhat even now. Improvement in the annual reporting of foundation activities is taking place, and it seems probable that the aggregate of foundation assets and of their annual disbursements for higher education will continue to grow.

Business and industrial corporations. People have long been accustomed to the idea of some contributions to higher education from philanthropic foundations, but only in recent years has there

---

[1] The grand total of charitable trusts extant in the United States probably exceeds 10,000. Most of them, however, are comparatively small.

been any substantial development of the concept of the business corporation as a source of gifts. Such corporations, organized for the purpose of providing profit for their stockholders, had not usually been thought of as donors of any part of their assets.

In fact, a decade ago there was serious doubt in the minds of lawyers and judges as to whether the board of directors of a business corporation possessed the authority to make any gifts without the consent of the stockholders. This doubt has been removed or greatly diminished by recent judicial decisions. A landmark was a New Jersey decision of 1953 regarding a gift made by a manufacturing corporation to Princeton University.[2]

The sound reasoning by which both the legality and the good policy of such gifts are sustained is based on several points. Corporations are large employers of educated personnel. They need to be assured of an adequate inflow of young men and women equipped to rise to positions of leadership. These come from the colleges, and more often from the liberal arts colleges and graduate schools than from the specialized technological schools.

Many corporation directors and officers believe that the existence and prosperity of the private colleges is an essential bulwark preventing unwanted encroachments by government—not only in the field of higher education but also in the sphere of business and industry. Furthermore, corporation managers keenly aware of the importance of good public relations know that a large amount of favorable publicity and local good will can be economically purchased by means of gifts to colleges.

Thus the sums spent in this manner are at least as justifiable as are the vast amounts expended annually for advertising. Corporations recognize obligations as citizens of the communities in which their plants are located and in the states where their operations are carried on. These obligations include the responsibility of contributing to the local charitable enterprises, among which colleges are properly numbered. Long ago the wiser among the directors of business corporations forsook the buccaneering policy of "the public be damned," and the old accusation that "corporations have no souls" is no longer often heard. Instead, the corporation now plays the role of public benefactor in more ways than one.

[2] *A. P. Smith Manufacturing Company* v. *Barlow*, 97 A. 2d 186, *affirmed*, 98 A. 2d 581 (New Jersey, 1953).

Volume and distribution. In 1954 a total of 728 reporting institutions of higher education received a grand total of $336 million in gifts; over $39 million came from business corporations. It is known that corporation giving has increased at a rapid rate since then. Among companies then aiding higher education, 73 per cent were including technical schools as recipients; 72 per cent, private universities; 71 per cent, liberal arts colleges; 52 per cent, professional schools; 47 per cent, state universities; and 15 per cent, junior colleges.

Expressing their preferences as to the allocation of their gifts, about 42 per cent of these companies favored giving to current operating funds; about 20 per cent, capital funds; about 19 per cent, student aid; and about 19 per cent, other special services.

Support from church organizations. Denominational or church-connected colleges and universities vary widely as to the closeness of their denominational ties and the volume of support they receive from the church. In the case of the Roman Catholic institutions, substantial support generally comes in the form of unsalaried services by members of the religious orders, who often compose all or a majority of the faculties, though in some instances they are a minority. Among the Protestant institutions there seems to have been a long-term tendency for the sectarian influence to weaken and for the religious support to become somewhat more attenuated than formerly.

This tendency is probably more evident among the larger urban church-related universities than among the smaller colleges, though there are many exceptions. It also appears to be true that in general the smaller Protestant denominations produce substantially larger annual contributions per church member for their colleges than do the larger denominations. For the largest church organizations the practicable goal seems to be perhaps $1 or $2 per member per year, while for some of the smaller ones with only a few thousand members and supporting only one or a few small colleges, the quota has been known to reach as much as $15 to $20 per member per year.

Local community sources. A respectable and flourishing college is a very important economic and cultural asset to any local community. It tends to produce educated manpower for the local industries and professions as well as for the state and the nation. It usually attracts at least a few students and faculty members from distant places who bring with them purchasing power to stimulate the local economy. Its payroll helps to stimulate local business. In a small town, its payroll may be as large as that of any other single business or industry in the vicinity.

Its presence usually affords a priceless opportunity for at least some young people in the immediate locality to attend college who would not be financially able to do so at all if they had to leave home and incur the expenses of travel and separate maintenance. It brings to the community at least a few really distinguished persons as faculty members or as occasional lecturers. It adds to the library resources of the locality, and stimulates in numberless ways the whole range of local cultural activities.

These matters are constantly becoming better understood by businessmen and industrialists, local professional people, labor organizations, and farmers. All these, as well as other local persons, can be sources of private gifts in various forms. It is likely that many of these are embraced in the category "nonalumni individuals," shown as the second largest source of private gifts in Table 4.

The college-and-community ties grow stronger and the prospects of local private support become better because of a long-term tendency for larger and larger proportions of high school graduates to attend college within commuting distance of their homes if possible. This trend will undoubtedly be accelerated as the total number of students increases and as new small colleges and junior colleges are established to make higher education accessible to more people.

Alumni gifts. Most college graduates have a strong sentimental attachment to their alma mater. During their college years they made many lifelong friendships and spent many of the happiest and most productive hours of their lives. They remember the place and the people with nostalgic affection. They enjoy revisiting the scene at alumni reunions. They like to receive the alumni magazine which gives them news of current campus activities and inklings of the current whereabouts and activities of their own former classmates.

Almost all institutions have an alumni association which annually elects not only its own officers but often also some alumni representatives to the governing board of the college. Most institutions also publish an alumni magazine to serve as a medium of communication and hold annual alumni ceremonies on campus, during which all former students are especially invited to revisit the scenes of their college days.

As long ago as 1870 William Graham Sumner, eminent professor of political and social science, wrote in enthusiastic advocacy of widespread contributions of modest gifts by large numbers of alumni:

> If every graduate who could afford it should give the college ten dollars, and others should give more in proportion, we should enter upon a plan whose financial soundness is unquestionable. We should be paying a debt which we all owe.

In 1890 Yale established the first alumni fund for annual giving. Dartmouth organized one in 1906. Wesleyan University began a similar scheme in 1915. The movement grew in the 1920's, but its greatest expansion has been more recent. In 1937 alumni funds in 86 institutions reported total gifts of less than $3 million for that year. In 1953, institutions numbering 302 reported just under $40 million; and in 1956, a total of 442 colleges and universities received alumni fund gifts of over $106 million.

Advantages of annual alumni giving. It is sometimes said that one of the merits of the plan is in the fact that it usually brings in unrestricted funds; that is, money that can be spent for any purpose the college chooses. But this statement needs some qualification: there is a tendency for alumni, like all donors in general, to respond well to a definite campaign for capital funds. For this reason, at least one institution is known to stipulate that half of the receipts from its alumni fund will be allocated to capital outlay and half to current operation.

In other cases efforts have been made to appeal to alumni for capital funds one year and for operating funds the next, thus alternating the two drives to keep them from interfering with each other. Probably this is no longer very widely done, but a new rationale of calling for restricted gifts has come into the picture: faculty salaries are so notoriously low in many of the smaller private colleges that some annual alumni fund campaigns are now directed exclusively to raising money to increase faculty salaries. This, however, is not an onerous restriction for faculty salaries always constitute the main element of annual operating expense (usually from 50 to 70 per cent) and therefore gifts earmarked for that purpose can hardly be the cause of any inconvenience to the institution.

The principal advantage of annual alumni giving is that it amounts to "living" endowment. Having a high degree of dependability from year to year, it can be relied upon apparently with as much confidence as can the income from invested endowments. Annual gifts aggregating $1 million are the equivalent of the income of an endowment of $25 million or more. The $106 million of alumni fund gifts received by 442 institutions in 1956 were equal to the returns of an endowment of the order of $3 billion.

There are further advantages. Alumni who have established a habit of annual giving tend to take an increasingly benevolent proprietary interest in the welfare and progress of the college. They defend its program, broadcast its needs, and herald its opportunities; and they are much more likely than others to make eventually a substantial gift or bequest to the institution in their later years.

The board of trustees as a source of support. A good deal has been said and written about the desirable qualifications for membership on a college or university governing board, as well as about the proper duties of such a member. Henry M. Wriston, president first of Lawrence College and then of Brown University, has coined a cogent apothegm: the member should bring to his board "work, wealth and wisdom." Each of these has bearing upon financial support, for "work" may at least in part take the form of soliciting gifts from affluent sources and "wisdom" may in part be applied as advice regarding the prudent and productive management of invested funds as well as advice concerning other aspects of the college operation.

An anonymous quotation is also circulated to the effect that a college trustee should "give, get, or get out"—which puts the idea in very blunt terms. The implication that a trustee should be able to make large gifts himself and/or influence his wealthy friends to do so is in accord with the facts of life regarding the survival of charitable enterprises in a pluralistic society; and it is said that college trustees have probably been responsible for as much as a third of the total of private gifts received.

In some quarters it is bitterly argued that almost all boards of trustees are heavily overweighted with bankers, financiers, and reactionary men of wealth, and that this tends to stifle academic freedom and retard the development of an altruistic and enlightened social philosophy in the colleges. Influence accompanies wealth, but not all affluent persons are reactionary or dictatorial. Since education cannot be a quick-profit enterprise or even a breakeven undertaking; it requires heavy investment by private donors as well as by the general public from tax sources.

Student Fees

It is possible to think of education as a service which should be bought and sold under private contract, at whatever price the market will bear. Proprietary schools necessarily operate on that principle because generally they have no source of income other than student fees. It goes without saying that in such institutions the student must pay the full cost of the instruction he gets, plus some profit for the purveyor.

Virtually all higher education in the United States is on a different basis.[3] Currently about 42 per cent of it (in terms of numbers of students) is offered by private nonprofit institutions chartered as charitable corporations, and about 58 per cent is offered by public institutions which are agencies of governmental units—usually the state.

Almost all the private institutions charge fees for tuition and other services, but seldom if ever do the tuition fees equal the cost of the educational service the student receives. The average private institution receives only about 55 per cent of its total operating income from student fees. Public establishments derive, on the average, only about 18 per cent of their total operating income from student fees. In some states the state universities and colleges are required by law to provide free tuition, but nearly all of these now charge at least nominal fees for other services—matriculation fees, health service fees, and so on. The public junior colleges in California are required by the state constitution to be free of fees.

Thus, with few exceptions, all types of institutions currently charge some fees. Moreover, the trend of fees has been upward for

[3] This omits the substantial amount of service at the level of higher education rendered in corporation training programs for present or prospective employees. These programs are proprietary, but most of the trainees are not customarily included in nationwide statistics of higher education.

two decades. For example, a survey of 196 universities and colleges indicated that the average of fees per student rose from $168 in 1940 to $249 in 1950 to $311 in 1955—an increase of 85 per cent over the whole period of fifteen years. For 76 private institutions the fees went up from $310 to $465 to $590 for a total increase of 90 per cent; and for 120 public institutions the rise was from $78 to $112 to $135 for a total increase of 73 per cent.[4] When one observes that this took place during an inflationary period in which the productivity of endowments had already been sharply reduced, one may well conclude that the increase in student fees was a necessity for the private institutions. For the public colleges and universities the situation is not so clear. With an average of 72 per cent of their operating revenues coming from governmental sources, they would not be completely devastated by the reduction or abolition of student fees. Although fees form a substantial sliver of their income, they have by no means shaken off the traditions of free tuition, and it is particularly apposite to argue that the public junior colleges should be as free of fees as are the public high schools.

This comes close to a view of education contrary to that stated in the first sentence of this section. It is possible to think of school or college attendance, not as a privilege for which the student must pay, but as a form of public service (much like military service) to which he is morally obligated if he is adjudged physically and mentally fit for it. Under this view higher education is worth its full cost to the state and the nation in terms of its results in enhanced national security and the building up of the national economy. Probably no one supposes that college and university attendance should be made compulsory, but there is very serious question as to whether any barriers—in the form of fees—should be maintained at the campus gates.

The tendency of public institutions to raise fees is no doubt partly owing to the fact that administrators and teachers in private and public institutions belong to the same national professional associations, read the same professional journals, and constantly mingle in conferences large and small for the discussion of problems of higher education. The raising of fees has apparently been inescapable for

[4] Ernest V. Hollis and Herbert S. Conrad, "Trends in Tuition Charges and Fees," *Annals of the American Academy of Political and Social Science,* 301 (September, 1955), 148–65.

most of the private institutions, and has had a large part in many writings and discussions related to their problems. Many of the public establishments have gone along with the movement, sometimes in the interest of additional income and perhaps sometimes in the interest of maintaining the shifting balance between student numbers at private and public institutions—or at least moderating the speed of the shift.[5] For three hundred years private colleges had at least a majority of all students in the United States. After about 1930 the division was more or less even and it oscillated somewhat for a decade or two before the swing to the public side began in earnest. Currently the proportions are about 42 per cent in private institutions and 58 per cent in public institutions. And the disparity is almost sure to increase.

Endowment as a Source of Income

A donor may stipulate that his gift is to constitute a perpetual fund, of which the principal (or *corpus*) is to be held forever intact, and only the income is to be expended.

Such a gift creates a charitable trust in perpetuity, a creature of equity jurisprudence. The instrument setting up the trust may be a deed of gift or a will. Unless it names a special trustee, the governing board of the beneficiary institution in its corporate capacity becomes the trustee of the fund. It is charged with the duty of conserving it, managing it in such a way as to produce maximum income consonant with safety, and expending the income for the charitable purposes defined in the trust instrument.

In theory, and in the eyes of the law, this solemn responsibility continues unto the end of time. Gifts of this kind are not touched by the rule against perpetuities, a universal principle of Anglo-American law which invalidates and renders illegal a trust in perpetuity intended for the exclusive benefit of named private persons and their descendants or successors. Such is a *private* trust, as distinguished from a *charitable* trust, which is for the benefit of an indefinite class of persons (such as the student-body of a college).

One landmark in the history of the definition of charitable trusts

[5] Some state legislators who have close ties with private institutions, and many who regard raises in fees as less politically hazardous than additional taxes, have taken attitudes tending to compel state universities and colleges to increase fees.

is the Statute of 43 Elizabeth (1602) in which the English Parliament specified education as one of the legitimate purposes of such a trust. Another is the opinion handed down by Chief Justice Gray of Massachusetts in 1869, when he defined a charitable trust as a gift to be administered:

> . . . consistently with existing laws, for the benefit of an indefinite number of persons either by . . . education or religion, or by relieving their bodies from disease, . . . or by assisting them to establish themselves in life; or by creating or maintaining public buildings or works; or by otherwise lessening the burdens of government.

Endowment funds are invested in farm lands, urban business properties, government bonds, utility bonds, the capital stock of business corporations, and in other forms. The rentals, interest, or dividends which accrue from these holdings become available for current expenditure by the beneficiary institution.

The most important fact to be noted about endowments in the period between 1925 and 1950 is that their productivity was cut in half by a great and apparently permanent decline in interest rates, so that an average return of 3 per cent was about all that could be expected in the late 1940's and early 1950's. Also, during and after this period, price inflation greatly reduced the purchasing power of the dollar, so that the real income from endowment has decreased by a great deal more than one half.

This is serious, even for the few wealthy colleges and universities whose endowments run into many millions. The situation could be disastrous for the great number of colleges whose endowments are slender if they do not struggle valiantly to make up the loss by increasing their annual volume of gifts for current expenditures, and by every other available means.

Indeed, the situation has brought about a considerable decline in the degree of professional and public approval of endowment as a means of financing higher education. There have always been some qualms among social philosophers regarding the desirability of accumulating great pools of wealth in the form of perpetual trusts, and to these theoretical objections are now added the practical dilemmas of college administrators who are forced to find other expedients if their institutions are to survive.

CHAPTER III

Where the Money Comes From: Income from Tax Sources

Under the American federal system there are three levels of government: local, state, and federal or national. Each level of government has the authority to levy taxes. This makes the total picture of taxation quite complicated. It was much less complex in earlier days, when most of the wealth of the nation was in the form of farms, homes, and small businesses. Then the property tax, levied in small local units for both local and state purposes, was a mainstay of the system. The federal government drew most of its comparatively small revenues from such sources as customs duties and excise taxes. There was little if any overlapping of federal and state taxes.

Within the last half-century all this has enormously changed. With the shift from an agricultural to an industrial economy, personal income—whether derived from salaries and wages or from rents, interest, and dividends—became a much more realistic measure of taxpaying ability than was mere ownership of property. Today a man owning a farm worth $100,000 may perhaps have a net annual income no larger than that of a skilled laborer who owns no property at all. A retired person owning a valuable home may have an income far lower than that of a garbage collector who owns none.

Huge corporations operate sprawling industrial and commercial empires with plants scattered throughout the country and, in numerous cases, throughout the world. Their branches have to a great extent supplanted local small business, even in small towns. Their ownership is to a considerable degree decentralized: it lies in the hands of millions of shareholders who derive income from their shares. But these shares are an incorporeal form of property easily moved from place to place and easily concealed. The management of these corporations is concentrated in the hands of a comparatively small managerial caste whose hugely swollen salaries and bonuses are tapped for substantial revenue under federal and state taxes on personal income.

A great and growing mass market for the products of assembly-line efficiency provides abundant profits for the corporations, so that a corporate income tax as well as a personal income tax is essential. The federal government levies both of these. The personal income tax is set at comparatively high rates and on a steeply progressive scale. Thus it has come about that the income tax is the principal source of federal revenue. The unprecedented federal expenditures for defense, foreign aid, interest on the national debt, maintenance of the domestic functions of the federal government, and grants-in-aid to the states for state functions such as highway construction, social welfare, public health, and education have caused the fiscal operations of the national government to overshadow those of the states and the local governments combined.

Some thirty-five or more of the states have also entered the personal and corporate income tax field, and the others will probably soon follow. In a few instances cities have been allowed to levy income taxes.

The federal government also levies taxes on the transfer of estates and gifts, and the states levy various forms of succession taxes—chiefly inheritance taxes.

The Complicated Backdrop of the Revenue System

A wide view of the taxation picture at all three levels of government discloses a good deal of complexity and some overlapping. Yet the picture is not as muddled as it might be, even though it was designed piecemeal rather than according to one basic blueprint.

The main features of the tax system at present may easily be outlined in a few bold strokes. By far the most important type of tax is the income tax. This is the source of much of the money expended under the huge federal budget.

The largest single source of state revenue is currently the sales tax, which may be "special" (for example, restricted to gasoline sales) or "general" (on all retail sales). A broader type of general sales tax is sometimes called a "gross income" tax. Some thirty-five states now have general sales taxes. Based as they are on the volume of daily transactions, these taxes are large and prompt producers of revenue. They spread rapidly among the states during the depression of the 1930's, when swift and substantial additions to the shrinking state revenues became imperative.

State income taxes are a second important source of state revenue. Some states derive considerable revenue from severance taxes or natural resources taxes levied on the extraction of oil or minerals or on the harvesting of timber. Practically all states levy special sales taxes on gasoline, liquor, and tobacco. Ad valorem taxes on property, once the chief source of state and local revenues, are still levied everywhere, but there seems to be a marked and growing trend for the states to leave all the revenues from this source in the hands of the local subdivisions.

Even where they have exclusive benefit of property taxes (whose rates are often limited by the state constitutions), counties, cities, and districts generally receive help for the maintenance of the local public services in the form of grants-in-aid from the state. For example, slightly more than half of the $2 billion budget for the state of New York for 1959–60 was for aid to local communities. The proportion is smaller in some of the less-developed states; but in the nation as a whole, the states now pay an average of about 40 per cent of the operating expenses of local public school districts out of state funds. Many states also make grants to local subdivisions for necessary capital outlays.

Thus the exercise of the power to levy taxes tends to move upward to the larger units (the states and especially the federal government). This necessitates the growth of subsidies from the larger units to the smaller ones in order to maintain local government and to avoid centralizing control of public services in the national capital. These are the reasons why the federal government makes grants to the states and why the states appropriate aid to their local subdivisions. These are also the reasons why massive federal aid to the states for education is eventually inevitable.

Support from Local Taxing Units

City or municipal universities and colleges are not numerous, but there are a few. These derive most of their support from city tax funds. All local public junior colleges, by definition, get some of their support from tax funds levied in the school districts, counties, or other local subdivisions in which they are located.

One curious form of local governmental contribution was widespread during the nineteenth century. Whenever a state institution was to be founded, counties and cities were encouraged to compete with each other in the matter of providing a free site plus a substantial sum of money. In several cases the state supreme courts upheld local bond issues or local tax levies undertaken for this purpose.

From the viewpoint of a statewide system, the results of this free-for-all rivalry were often weird. More than once two major state institutions were placed within a few miles of each other, while other areas in the same state had no institution at all. The theory was that competition would solve all the problems of a free society and that centralized planning was neither necessary nor desirable. The same spirit was exhibited toward the founding of private institutions—but the state courts often struck down, on obvious constitutional grounds, local tax levies or bond issues undertaken in these cases. There was nothing, however, to prevent the raising of funds by private subscription, and this was often done. Indeed, subscriptions or gifts were sometimes conditioned upon the location of the institution. This circumstance sometimes caused difficulties when at some later time it appeared desirable to move the institution to a new location.

Municipal universities and colleges. New York and Ohio are among the few states having municipal institutions. Others are Kentucky, Kansas, and Nebraska. The four city colleges in New York City were municipally supported until relatively recently, but the state now subsidizes the parts of their programs which pertain directly to the education of teachers and also the first two years of the general program. This aid, though substantial, is only a minor part of the total budgets of these institutions; the major part of their support continues to come from city tax revenues. The municipal universities of Cincinnati, Toledo, and Akron in Ohio are city-supported. Municipal colleges generally charge no tuition fees to residents of the city, and their fees for other services are comparatively low. In many cases they owe their origin to a local desire to extend free public education upward to include the university level.

This is the same urge that gave impulse to the founding of many of the state universities, colleges, and normal schools.

Local public junior colleges. Often the community junior college simply emerges as the thirteenth and fourteenth grades in a local public school district, and that taxing unit is its primary source of support. Sometimes the junior college occupies assigned rooms or entire buildings formerly used by the high school. This is not, however, an optimum physical plant for junior college purposes. Not only should the college have its own campus and buildings (including especially a suitable library building), but it should also have its own operating budget adjusted to junior college purposes and needs.

These considerations have helped to bring about the systems of state subsidies for junior college plant outlays, and schemes of state subvention of junior college annual operating budgets. The amount of state aid per college student per year should be at least somewhat larger than the rate per high school student. It is also essential that the number of seats in the library reading-room in proportion to total enrollment be much larger than in traditional residence colleges, because nearly all students will commute and many of them can spend only a few hours per day on the campus. The same considerations apply to the fixing of local tax rates and the formulation of local school system budgets when the system includes a junior college. The trend of state subsidies is upward, but this does not mean that the trend of local support is or can be downward. A great merit of the community junior college is that it is primarily a local institution, locally controlled and at least in substantial part locally supported.

Some junior colleges are units in the local school system operated by a board of education; others stand alone to serve districts set up especially for junior college purposes and have their own boards. Variations also exist as to the status of municipal universities and colleges. Regardless of all these diversities, it is profitable to consider for a moment the kind of performance and the types of public relations that encourage good support from a local governmental subdivision. These will be discussed only briefly, because in many respects they are not widely different from the principles applicable to the cultivation of state support.

Most of the students in a locally-supported college live within a few miles of its campus. Such a college has the advantage of a compact clientele on a community basis. The "neighborhood" atmosphere is much more predominant in a small city than in a large one. A county seat with its surrounding trade area (which sometimes exceeds the boundaries of the county) tends to become knit into a single community, served by a local newspaper and one radio station. The differences between farm people and town people are minimized.

The county seat has the traditional courthouse offices, including those of the county board of education and the county health board, and it also usually has the local outposts of the principal state and federal public services, such as the public employment service, the agricultural extension service, the soil conservation service, the social welfare office, and others. It has a local chamber of commerce, various service clubs composed of local businessmen, the county headquarters of great farm organizations (such as the Farm Bureau and the Grange), many labor union locals, and often a county council of labor organizations.

Mobilizing good will. All these are agencies through which a vast amount of community good will can be generated. The administrators and the faculties of locally-supported colleges should miss no opportunity to mingle with the leaders and members of reputable local organizations. They can address meetings when requested, render a great variety of consultative services, and—in appropriate cases—accept responsibilities as regular officers or committee members of the local organizations.

In the case of the small local public college, members of the faculty have opportunity to visit students' homes and to receive their parents frequently as guests of the college. When the college's annual request for appropriations comes to the local board of education or other taxing body, as the case may be, very probably some of these same parents or some of the members of the local organizations will be members of the appropriating body. Their favorable views of the college and its job will be backed up by their neighbors who are also parents, members of the local organizations, readers of the local newspaper, and listeners to the local radio programs.

All this applies equally well to a private college, the only difference being that the goal in that case is a good flow of private gifts and subscriptions instead of a public appropriation of tax money. Public colleges, too, can benefit from private gifts, as witness Flint

Junior College in Michigan, which has an endowment of $5 million and several valuable buildings received from private sources.

Public relations is not to be thought of as a bag of tricks. It must be based on sound service, which means the college must maintain instruction of good quality, strive to keep its program ahead of the development of the community, and be forthright in its dealings with the public. It should study its prospective students, survey the industries and professions of the community, and study the careers of its graduates. From such efforts come the data which provide convincing support of requests for appropriations of local tax money, as well as gifts and other forms of support.

The land-grant college and the community. Every state has at least one land-grant institution, state-controlled and state-supported,[1] which is a link in the nationwide agricultural extension service operated and supported jointly by the federal government, the state, and the county. Most counties have from one to four or more persons, headed by the county agricultural extension agent, on permanent duty in the county. Staff members often include a county home demonstration agent (a woman trained in home economics), an associate or assistant county agricultural agent, and an assistant for boys' and girls' clubs.

The land-grant institution in each state, in addition to having a network of county agricultural extension offices in the county seats, ordinarily maintains a traveling staff of extension specialists who are available for various meetings and demonstrations for groups of farmers and housewives at the request of the county agents. Thus a considerable proportion of the people of every county have face-to-face contacts not only with the local agents, but also with traveling representatives of the institution. These direct contacts with the people of the state are of great advantage to the land-grant institution in maintaining a climate favorable to support.

The county tax contributions to this service constitute only a small part of the income of the institution. For example, in 1957–58, county support for agricultural extension services amounted to 2.2 per cent of the operating income of Ohio State University.

---

[1] In New York the state-supported colleges of agriculture, home economics, veterinary medicine, and industrial and labor relations at Ithaca are entrusted to the administration of the board of trustees of Cornell University, a privately controlled institution.

This percentage is somewhat larger in the case of some of the smaller land-grant colleges in other states, particularly where the land-grant institution is distinct from the state university.

Support from the States

It is the separate states which charter practically all the private and public institutions of higher education. The federal government enters this part of the picture only to an infinitesimal extent, chiefly in the District of Columbia and other federal areas, except in the case of the national academies for the education of career officers in the major branches of the armed services.

State support of private institutions. In Colonial times it was not uncommon for public funds to be appropriated by the colonial or local legislative bodies for the support of private colleges. In fact, there were then in existence none but private colleges, and the concept of the public college or university as known today was undeveloped. Therefore no distinction needed to be made between private and public institutions.

Harvard College in the seventeenth and eighteenth centuries received public aid from the Colony and from various town treasuries, and from the Commonwealth of Massachusetts up to 1823. One of its affiliated corporations, the Museum of Comparative Zoology, received grants from the Commonwealth in later years. New Hampshire did not finally discontinue legislative appropriations to Dartmouth College until 1920.

Nearly all the state constitutions, except those of a few states in the New England and Middle Atlantic regions, now prohibit appropriations of public money to any institution not under the control of the state. The constitution of Massachusetts was amended to that effect in 1917. Pennsylvania's constitution was construed for forty years as permitting state aid to private and denominational colleges, and by 1919 the annual total of such appropriations was over $2 million. In 1921 a notable decision of the state court of last resort cut off all state support to denominational colleges, but allowed it to continue for private nonsectarian institutions. To this day the University of Pennsylvania, Temple University, and the University of Pittsburgh, as well as several other private institutions (chiefly medical colleges) receive state appropriations. A decision of 1925 also declared that the state is prohibited from making any contract with a sectarian institution which requires expenditure of state funds.

The Maryland constitution has never been held to prohibit state support of private nonsectarian institutions, and there is a long, though somewhat intermittent, history of state grants to Johns Hopkins University and a few other private colleges in the state.

It is noteworthy that in the period immediately following World War I some states enacted "educational bonus laws" whereby payments to cover subsistence and books were made to the eligible veterans who attended college, and payments were made to the college to cover the actual increased cost incurred by the attendance of the veterans. In Wisconsin such a statute was held to be no violation of the constitution, because "mere reimbursement is not aid." It is also well known that for many years New Jersey contracted with private colleges and paid for their services in lieu of the establishment of a state university. Florida currently pays the University of Miami, a private institution, $3000 a year to compensate for the cost of instructing each Florida student enrolled in its medical college.

Exemption from state taxes. Every state without exception exempts private and public colleges from state and local taxation, at least to a substantial extent. Public institutions are, with the rarest exceptions, wholly exempt. In all states private colleges are exempt from property taxes—at least on property owned, occupied, and used for educational purposes—and in some states they are also exempt from taxes on funds and property held as endowment. Donors to either type of institution generally may deduct the value of their gifts and bequests from their taxable estates, and from their taxable incomes under state income tax laws.

Educational institutions are also exempted, to varying degrees, from numerous other types of state and local taxes. All this adds up to the equivalent of a substantial state subsidy to private colleges as well as to public establishments. A detailed examination of the subject would necessarily be lengthy and complex. Suffice it to say here that tax exemption of private institutions rests upon sound theory: they perform indispensable public services which would otherwise have to be paid for out of tax revenues.

State support of public institutions. Appropriations by the state legislatures are now the principal source of operating funds for state-controlled colleges and universities, but no state institution gets all its support in that manner, and the proportions of the total income coming from that source vary greatly.

The practice of making regular annual or biennial appropriations to the state establishments of higher education did not become customary until after the Civil War. Prior to that time, the institutions—even though established and controlled by the state—were largely left to fend for themselves with the aid of an occasional state loan or a statutory authorization to operate a lottery to raise funds. Appropriations, when and where they were made, were small and sporadic. This accords with the fact that many of the state institutions were regarded as private corporations, and the theory of higher education as a state function had not been firmly developed everywhere.

After the policy of regular periodic appropriations took root, the size of the appropriations grew with the size of the institutions, and for a time many of the states levied taxes and earmarked the revenues for higher education. These were generally taxes on property and were commonly called "millage" taxes. They did not eliminate the necessity of making regular periodic appropriations out of the general fund, but they provided a backlog of revenue for each fiscal period, which could be supplemented by current appropriations. The practice has declined, partly because of the diminishing role of property taxes in state revenue. In some instances, as in Louisiana, a millage tax for higher education is authorized by the state constitution.

Several other state services have since about 1915 greatly increased their relative shares of state expenditures, due partly to the use of allocated taxes (such as a gasoline tax for highways), and partly to proffered subsidies from the federal government which the states must match out of state funds. The vast development of highway systems and social welfare services has caused the share of state funds allotted to higher education to shrink relatively (but of course not absolutely). It has been shown that the percentage of all state expenditures going for higher education has dropped from 10 per cent in 1915 to about 4 per cent in the 1950's. During the same period total state expenditures increased about seventeen-fold, with public welfare expenditures growing fifty-fold, and outlays for higher education increasing only eleven-fold.

It cannot be known with certainty whether the relative growth in state expenditures for social welfare and highways has reached its peak, but it is certain that oncoming increases in student enrollment during the next fifteen years will call for correspondingly substantial increases in the amounts of state expenditures for higher education.

This situation requires a searching study of state revenue systems, because it is very probable that the people will decide to support higher education generously. The possibilities of augmented state revenues, of increased support from private sources, and of massive federal aid to the states must also be examined.

State contributions to the support of community colleges. Those local junior colleges that are merely branches of a state university or integral parts of a consolidated state system of higher education receive no local tax support. The larger proportion of the public community colleges, however, is based on a local taxing unit (school district or junior college district) from which they receive their primary support, though not necessarily a major part of it. The percentages vary considerably, but it appears that the average community college generally receives about one third of its operating funds from the state, one third from local taxation, and one third from student fees. State aid to community colleges generally follows the schemes previously worked out for aid to public school districts, and usually is largely in the form of a fixed amount for each student in average daily attendance. This amount currently varies in different states from about $150 to $400 per year per student.

In addition, some of the states provide for state contributions for capital outlays, often by a lump appropriation for the fiscal period, which is to be allocated to community college districts which can match the state funds with local funds. These contributions are made in the order in which the districts apply until the state funds are exhausted.

In considering the nationwide panorama, it is well to remember that even now only about half the states have developed a statewide network of local community junior colleges on any considerable scale. California is far in the lead, and Texas is second.

State support of state institutions. State appropriations to Ohio State University in 1957–58 constituted 46.3 per cent of the university's total income for educational and general purposes for that year. This percentage also tends to run somewhat higher in the case of smaller and newer state-supported institutions in Ohio and other states, especially the western states.

The meagerness or abundance of the annual or biennial appropriations made by the legislature depends upon a complex of factors only partly susceptible of being immediately influenced by the institutions of higher education. Economic conditions at the time have important bearings on the prospect. For example, during the great depression of the 1930's, the tax revenues of every state shrank alarmingly and the general atmosphere of apprehension was at first almost paralyzing. Budgets were drastically reduced. Dismissal of junior faculty members in droves and salary cuts for all employees were the order of the day. Some literal-minded and straight-faced educators developed a literature of "economies" in operation, and devoted pamphlets or whole books to such matters as turning off the lights when not in use, keeping the windows closed to save fuel, reducing the open hours of libraries, cutting down the services of cleaning and sanitation, ad infinitum and ad nauseam.

Yet there was soon a rebound from the downward slide. In the early and middle 1930's, state after state introduced the large and swift income-producing general sales tax in some form, which served to increase—often almost to double—their revenues. New or revised income taxes also played a part in some states, and now more than twenty states have both income taxes and general sales taxes. Often a good deal of the new income had to go to public school districts and other local subdivisions so that teachers whose salaries were months in arrears could be paid and given some assurance that they would be paid in the future, though usually at rates even lower than the meager sums specified in their contracts.

The stringency made inevitable great forward strides in the modernization of state taxing systems and state plans for the financing of local public schools. State institutions of higher education shared to some extent in the improved situation and began a long upward movement from the panic level of the early depression years.

Access to legislative halls. Each state has one institution which is unquestionably its principal state university. In about twenty states this principal university is not the land-grant institution, which is located on a different campus in another part of the state. Traditionally, there has been intense competition between the two. In most instances the land-grant college is nearly equal to (and in a few cases exceeds) the state university in number of students, size of plant, and volume of financing. Many of the land-grant colleges have become cosmopolitan universities with a dozen or more major schools and divisions specializing in agriculture, veterinary medicine, basic arts and sciences, business administration, engineering, forestry, home economics, pharmacy, and other disciplines. The land-grant institution usually does not have schools of law or of medicine; the state university, on the other hand, does nothing or only comparatively little in the fields of agriculture, home economics, and veterinary medicine. Both types of institutions offer graduate courses in their respective fields of emphasis, but the state university usually offers a larger and superior selection than does the land-grant college.

The free-for-all rivalry for the favor of the public and of the legislature which characterized the early part of this century and which, to a considerable extent, continues even now has had many interesting results. For example, in Oregon a State Board of Higher Curricula to eliminate costly overlapping of curricular offerings was created as early as 1905 and functioned with a minimum of success until 1931. It was then replaced by the State Board of Higher Education, which was set up to be the sole governing board of all state-supported colleges and universities (then five in number).

During the period 1905–31, the struggle between the two principal institutions continued unabated. The land-grant college blanketed the state with its agricultural extension service and kept an additional corps of student-recruiters busy. The state university developed its own general extension service (a practice common in other states similarly situated), and had its own corps of recruiters. The presidents of both institutions, accompanied by staffs of senior professors and research assistants, took up residence in hotels at the state capital at the beginning of each legislative session and remained there until the session ended. The land-grant college gained an advantage from the fact that for a quarter of a century its president was a man of iron will and boundless energy who possessed every qualification for leadership in the state and who, in the course of his long tenure, built up a tremendous hold upon the good will of the public and of the legislature. During the same period, the state university had several short-term presidents, some of whom lacked the requisite physical stamina and the rough-and-tumble political know-how essential to success under those circumstances.

The long-run result was that both institutions received markedly generous support from the state, so that during the late 1920's and early 1930's Oregon led the states with from 30 to 35 per cent of the population of college age actually attending college—a figure which has not been reached by the nation as a whole even now, a full generation later. The land-grant college slightly exceeded the state university in size, enrollment, plant, and support; but both institutions grew, expanded their offerings and facilities, and provided the state with an almost unparalleled range of opportunities for higher education for its young people. Who shall say that this outcome of the brass-knuckled competition between the institutions was other than good?

The situation in Oregon was paralleled in many other states having vigorous land-grant colleges and equally viable "separated" state universities—among them, Washington, Utah, Colorado, Kansas, Iowa, Indiana, and Michigan. It is not to be inferred that these states are all alike as to higher education, for the differences are many. Michigan, most populous of the group, has a land-grant institution in the topmost rank of its kind and a state university second to none. These institutions remain unsurpassed even in equally populous states which combine state university and land-grant college in one institution.

Most of the states just mentioned have a spate of respectable institutions which originated as normal schools, became four-year teachers colleges, and in many cases now offer fifth-year work. Some of them have even acquired the title of "university." All these, of course, are in the competitive picture; but usually they have been somewhat overshadowed in the struggle between two titans, as was the case in Oregon.

Coordination of statewide systems.[2] From 1896 to 1948, a dozen states adopted the harsh expedient of abolishing the governing boards of all their state colleges and universities and setting up one statewide board to govern them all. Some twenty other states, while retaining separate governing boards for each of their major universities, have long had several of their smaller state colleges under one board—sometimes the state board of education. This trend is currently defunct.

Since 1941 a dozen other states, leaving their institutional boards intact, have set up a single statewide board either as a superimposed coordinating body or as an agency to afford lateral liaison among the several state institutions of higher education. The first of these boards (in Oklahoma) has power to allocate all state appropriations among the eighteen state colleges and universities; but no other board of this type has such authority, and there is a strong and continuing trend toward giving them only advisory duties (i.e., conduct studies and make recommendations). This is largely true of all such boards created during the late 1950's and early 1960's.

Meantime in several other states similar aims are advanced by the voluntary method; that is, a voluntary council of ranking representatives of all the state institutions maintains a small research staff and conducts studies and makes recommendations regarding the development of the statewide system. Such councils exist in Ohio, Indiana, Michigan, and Colorado. To some extent at least, voluntary coordination takes place in every state having more than one institution.

The authority of the governor and the state legislature to determine state appropriations is a forceful though sometimes blunt and ill-advised coordinating influence. In practically every state, under the state executive budget system, the state director of finance or state budget director takes a hand in the coordination of institutional budgets. Moreover, in some states certain statehouse functionaries are authorized to preaudit institutional expenditures,

---

[2] Much of the rationale of statewide planning is set forth in three recent publications: T. R. McConnell, *A General Pattern for American Public Higher Education* (New York: McGraw-Hill Book Company, Inc., 1962); Lyman A. Glenny, *Autonomy of Public Colleges: The Challenge of Coordination* (New York: McGraw-Hill Book Company, Inc., 1959); M. M. Chambers, *Voluntary Statewide Coordination in Public Higher Education* (Ann Arbor, Mich.: Publications Office of The University of Michigan, 1961).

operate a central office for the purchase of institutional supplies and equipment, execute or supervise the construction of institutional buildings, contract for or perform all printing and publishing for the institutions, or otherwise control phases of the institutional operations. That these too-tight administrative controls by statehouse offices are incompatible with efficiency in higher education has been lucidly set forth many times.[3]

Presenting the case for higher education. No attempt is here made to trace the diversity and complexity of the channels of state administrative organization through which the budgets of state institutions must go in the various states to culminate in an appropriation bill enacted by the legislature and signed by the governor. Instead, some principles of lobbying that will be applicable under almost any circumstances are presented.

Governmental practices have come a long way since the days when venality was almost common among the legislators and state administrative officers, when in many state capitals graft and corruption were rampant, and when it was not hard to find legislators who would accept bribes or who could be swayed by being plied with liquor and loose women. Those methods even yet occasionally break into the headlines, but more and more rarely. They are still used to some extent, especially in instances where large private profits are at stake in legislative or administrative matters; but unquestionably they are on the way out.

"Lobbying" has acquired new meanings. In great part it now consists of a straightforward marshaling and presentation of facts. Leading organizations of businessmen, professional people, farmers, and wage-earners maintain permanent secretariats at the state capital, where they work assiduously to collect and publish facts about their respective occupations, and to stimulate and assist their local units in the counties and cities in crystallizing and expressing their opinions. Commonly they receive and study sets of resolutions from their local units regarding issues of the day, and usually hold a convention of accredited delegates once a year to deliberate upon the issues and formulate the organization's position regarding them.

---

[3] Recent landmarks in this area are the reports of the Committee on Government and Higher Education, headed by Milton Eisenhower and financed by the Fund for the Advancement of Education: The Committee, *The Efficiency of Freedom* (Baltimore: Johns Hopkins Press, 1959) and Malcolm Moos and Francis E. Rourke, *The Campus and the State* (Baltimore: Johns Hopkins Press, 1959).

This then becomes the basis of their program for the year, to be pushed in the legislative session by the state secretariat. Many of the men and women on these secretariats or office staffs are well equipped by native ability and by education to do an excellent job of persuasion. They persuade the chairmen of legislative committees to schedule hearings on bills of special interest to them; they bring in delegations of members of their organizations from various parts of the state to testify at the hearings. They draft bills embodying policies of their organizations and persuade members of the legislature to introduce and sponsor them. They conduct radio and television broadcasting programs to inform and persuade the public regarding the issues. They become personally acquainted with legislators, often respond in person to their individual requests for information, and occasionally entertain them in large or small groups at modest dinners to which they sometimes bring their county and local chiefs from all parts of the state.

At its best, such an organization is an excellent tool of democratic and representative government, contributing to the catalyzing of public opinion by democratic methods, supplying the legislature with much authentic information and research service, and functioning as an effective sort of "third chamber" of the legislature. This is the rosy picture of modern lobbying.

At its worst such an organization may be a raucous purveyor of obviously biased propaganda, perhaps spending huge sums on high-pressure methods of influencing legislators, and not too meticulous about the ethics of its operations. It is this type of activity which had a part in impelling political scientists to label modern lobbying organizations "pressure groups" and to deplore the fact that even the best of them are so specialized in their viewpoint that there is really no broad-scaled lobby to represent the undivided interest of the public.

It is largely true also that a farmers' lobby, for instance, is rather likely to be supported, led, and dominated by comparatively substantial and prosperous farmers, while large numbers of small farmers remain aloof. By the same token, a business or industrial lobby is in danger of domination by one or a few titans. Professional lobbies, such as those conducted by physicians' associations, bar associations, and engineering societies, are generally notoriously hidebound in their social viewpoints—which may perhaps be taken as a sad commentary on the effectiveness of the liberal element in education in an earlier day. Lobbies of teachers and social workers are usually an exception to this tendency, since they often show at least some forward-looking propensities. But even they may let matters of self-interest, such as tenure and salaries, dominate their efforts.

So far as the existence of a permanent and aboveboard lobby on a statewide basis is concerned, the public elementary and secondary schools seem to be in advance of higher education. The National Education Association has in practically every state a strong constituent state education association which maintains a small but competent staff at the state capital, and is often able to rally to its support the statewide organization of Parent-Teacher Associations or the state branch of the American Association of University Women or the State Federation of Women's Clubs.

Most of the state education lobbies have already made substantial strides in getting state aid for local school districts, and they may be expected to improve in wisdom and effectiveness as time goes by. Every state college or university has an alumni association but, attached as they are to sentimental "institutionalism," there is danger that alumni may sometimes cancel each other's influence by being at loggerheads. Almost every state college or university has the advantage that its president is universally recognized as a highly reputable public figure to whom most legislators will listen with respect. The same is true to a somewhat lesser extent of most members of the governing boards, though they sometimes find it difficult to escape embroilment in personal or partisan politics in the state. The individuals differ considerably, of course, as to the degrees of respect and influence they can command.

College and university faculties have their intramural "senates" and councils and their local chapters of the American Association of University Professors,[4] but neither type of organization has any strong statewide focal center. There are "state academies of arts and sciences" and the like, but apparently they usually do little to try to influence legislation. In fact, their charters often proscribe and forbid such activities. Most of the myriad professional and scientific societies of professors are devoted to restricted fields and

---

[4] There are some state federations of AAUP chapters which may have potential for influencing legislation.

are heavily national or international in their purview, giving little attention to statewide affairs or statewide organization.

The relatively new Association for Higher Education, affiliated with the National Education Association, seems to be developing some statewide constituent organizations. The association is open to all ranks of professional employees of public and private institutions, from presidents to instructors, and its state organizations may eventually join forces with the state education associations in the support of an organization for the advancement of education at all levels. It may be noted with some satisfaction that at least some of the state education association lobbies have already adopted the practice of publicly supporting the budget requests of the state institutions of higher education.

Apparently state colleges and universities have no affiliated parents' organizations. In view of the sacrifices that many parents make to provide their children with a college education, and in view of the recurrent pressures upon legislators and board members to increase tuition fees, it may be wondered that parents do not become more vocal.

These are at present then only speculations about the possibility of organized lobbies for higher education. Next must be examined a few principles upon which the relations between higher education and the legislature can safely be based.

"Open covenants openly arrived at." There is a school of thought among college administrators to the effect that much of the institution's affairs ought to be kept secret from the public. A college business officer once said: "We don't want to put burglar tools in the hands of our enemies." Another college representative is said to have appeared before a legislative committee with a little black book which he held close to his chest, and answered questions by referring to the book. When a committee member asked if the members could have copies of the book, he hastily stammered, "No, this is the only copy there is."

Some administrators think that publication of faculty salaries will destroy faculty morale and cause internal dissension. It must be observed that in a state institution all these items are matters of public record to which any citizen, including newsmen, has a right of access. This also applies to the deliberations of the governing board at its meetings. A board may choose to hold an executive session (from which all nonmembers are excluded) on occasions when it wishes to discuss privately the personal qualifications of the president or of applicants for the presidency, or other emergency matters not appropriate for public release; but such a secret session should reach only an informal consensus rather than adopt formally any motion or resolution.

Much as one may deplore the proclivities of some legislators, executive officers, or members of the public to become entangled in minute details of institutional finance, and admit that at times the institution may suffer great detriment as a result of such meddling, a policy of secrecy or semisecrecy is not wise in the long run. It will inevitably generate suspicion and unfounded hostility which is likely to mount to harmful proportions. Americans are accustomed to know the salaries of their public officers and employees and the details about what goes on in their local legislative bodies and administrative boards. They rightly resent being told that "Papa knows best" in such matters.

Undue and morbid curiosity about details is usually largely forestalled by regular publication of carefully arranged financial reports which emphasize the major aspects of the operation and which are increasingly being accompanied by skillfully written but truthful and candid textual matter. The text is often interspersed with well-selected photographs and graphic illustrations which properly concentrate the reader's attention on the thrilling possibilities inherent in the various instructional undertakings and research projects, and expose for him some of the outlines of the future hoped for. Truth and candor must be the policy of a university: it has nothing to conceal.

The Federal Government's Participation

Even before the adoption of the Constitution of the United States, the Congress of the Confederation adopted the Northwest Ordinance regarding the government of the great territory which subsequently became the states of Ohio, Michigan, Indiana, Illinois, and Wisconsin. This provided for the reservation of designated public lands for the endowment of schools and seminaries of learning.

Ohio University at Athens (1802) and Miami University at Oxford, Ohio (1809) were the first state universities west of the

Appalachians. Each was the beneficiary of certain public lands, and each derives some income from that source to this day. After the admission of Ohio to the Union in 1803, it became the custom to write into the Enabling Acts (under which successive new states were admitted to the Union) provisions whereby the federal government granted public lands to the states for the endowment not only of a statewide system of public schools but also of a state university or several separate state institutions of higher education.

In some states much of the great potential income from the federal land grants was forever lost through public bungling or downright venality. But in many of the newer states of the west, the large land endowments already supply a larger share of the institutional income than is generally realized, and if they continue to be well managed they may produce much more in the future. The whole story of these federal land grants to the states for higher education would fill a large volume. Texas, after nine years as a sovereign nation, joined the Union in 1845 under an agreement whereby one million acres of public lands were reserved for the University of Texas. Oil royalties from some of these lands now add substantially to the income of the university.

There are also a few instances in the early nineteenth century wherein the federal Congress made outright appropriations of money to a private college, but this never took root as a custom and has long since been forgotten.

The Morrill Act and its train. During the decade of the 1850's there was an upsurge of sentiment for practical education in agriculture and the mechanic arts. About the middle of the decade, a few states, including Pennsylvania and Michigan, established farmers' colleges. In 1859 Congress passed a bill to grant federal public lands (or land scrip in lieu of lands) to every state which would agree to devote the income to at least one college of the new type. The bill was vetoed by President James Buchanan, but Senator Justin S. Morrill of Vermont continued to press for it and it was finally enacted and signed by President Abraham Lincoln in 1862.

During the ensuing half-century state after state accepted the act and executed it according to its terms. Some of the New England states designated a private institution as the land-grant college, but eventually they transferred the benefit to separately established state colleges of agriculture and engineering. In addition to the unique case of Cornell University in New York (see p. 37n), a single exception survives: Massachusetts Institute of Technology, a private institution which still receives one third of the benefits. (The remainder goes to the University of Massachusetts, which was until recently the state college of agriculture.)

Seventeen southern states each established two land-grant institutions, one for Negroes and one for white students. Land-grant institutions were also designated or established in the outlying territories of Alaska, Hawaii, and Puerto Rico, so that the total of these institutions came to 69. In about thirty instances the principal state university is now one and the same as the land-grant college; but in about twenty states the land-grant establishment and large state university are two separate institutions.

The Morrill Act of 1862 was followed by a chain of supplementary acts, extending down into the twentieth century. Notable were the Hatch Act of 1887, providing flat-rate appropriations of money to the states for agricultural experiment stations; and the Smith-Lever Act of 1914, providing for the beginnings of the cooperative federal-state-local agricultural extension service.

Depression and wartime measures. For several years (1935–41) the federal government allocated funds to public and private colleges and universities without distinction for the National Youth Administration student work program, under which large numbers of needy students who would not otherwise have been able to continue in school were employed part-time by the institution and permitted to earn about $180 per year. The jobs were of vast variety, ranging from garbage-hauling to assisting in advanced research. Many of the jobs for girls were clerical and stenographic, but the list also included hospital and laboratory assistants and many other types. Some professors and administrators were enthusiastic and thought this combining of work experience and education was helpful to all concerned; but others were annoyed by it and sniffed at "made work" and "leaf-raking."

World War II swept millions of young men into military service and many young women into defense industries, temporarily depleting college enrollments. In 1944, the famed G.I. Bill was enacted to provide subsistence and the cost of books and tuition in the school, college, or university of their choice to men and women honorably discharged from the armed forces. In each case, the duration of the period during which the provisions of the bill remained effective depended upon the length of wartime service. The several billions of dollars involved in this enterprise dwarfed all earlier federal expenditures connected with higher education. But the horde of veteran students who overwhelmed the colleges, bringing federal money with them, proved in general to be industrious and strongly motivated, giving the colleges an unaccustomed air of seriousness and maturity. The prevailing estimate of the whole undertaking is that it was an act of simple justice to the veterans and also a profitable investment from the standpoint of the nation's economy.

The most unfortunate results of the G.I. Bill were in the vocational education field. Considerable numbers of makeshift fly-by-night proprietary vocational schools were organized for the main purpose of obtaining the federal tuition payments by fraud, and they occasionally succeeded for a time. In the training-on-the-job phase of the program, some unscrupulous industrial employers sought to exploit the veterans by using them as cheap labor and providing little or nothing worthy of the name of instruction, for which the federal government was paying.

A program similar to the G.I. Bill was authorized for veterans of the Korean conflict and carried out with comparable success. It is not yet fully terminated. It differed from the G.I. Bill of 1944 in that instead of providing for payments from the government to the institutions, it provided only for somewhat larger allowances to the veterans, out of which they were to pay any tuition fees. This eliminated some of the incentives toward chicanery inherent in the earlier act.

Grants and loans for plant construction. During the depression of the 1930's Reconstruction Finance Corporation loans were made to universities for the erection of buildings, and the great lending agency known as the Public Works Administration for a time made a combination of loans and outright grants for public college plant construction.

During the war, construction—except for defense facilities—came to a halt; but immediately at the close of hostilities the vast influx of veterans and other students created such a housing stringency on the campus as had never been known before. Veterans often brought wives and babies with them. Here the federal government gave a helping hand in a somewhat novel way. Wooden barracks at the vast and hastily erected wartime cantonments were given or sold at nominal prices to the colleges, dismantled, and moved to the vicinity of the campus, where they were re-erected for use as residence facilities for students and their families. In many instances they were also used as temporary classrooms, laboratories, and office buildings. In several cases whole military stations or portions of them, sometimes of permanent construction, were vacated and turned over to some college or university for use as a branch institution to take care of the overflow of veterans.

During this same period large quantities of surplus material, useful as instructional equipment in engineering, shop, and science courses, was made available practically free of charge to universities, colleges, and schools. This included aircraft of various types, a great variety of electronic apparatus and instruments, internal combustion motors, and innumerable other items.

A new program of federal loans for student housing and related facilities was inaugurated in 1950 and extended to private institutions as well. Such institutions had not been eligible under the prewar program. In recent years, federal aid for the construction of medical school facilities has also been especially important.

Federal scholarships, fellowships, loans. In the late 1940's and early 1950's, as the operation of the G.I. Bill began to taper off, there was considerable advocacy of a federal program of scholarships and fellowships to take its place. The National Education Association and the U.S. Commissioner of Education helped to draft bills which were introduced in successive sessions of Congress; but none were enacted. One such bill, after having been pared down at the dictation of the Administration to exclude scholarships for undergraduates and to provide only for loans, plus fellowships for graduate students, was finally enacted in 1958 and signed by President Dwight D. Eisenhower. This is known as the National Defense Education Act of 1958 (see pp. 57, 66–69, 73).

Grants and contracts for research. A comparatively recent development is the awarding of grants and contracts to universities and colleges for research on a rapidly growing scale. Among the principal agencies are the Department of Defense, the National Aeronautics and Space Administration, the Atomic Energy Commission, the National Institutes of Health, the National Science Foundation, the Office of Education, and the Department of Agriculture. In 1959 nearly $500 million went from these agencies to universities for research grants and contracts.[5]

Problems connected with the equitable financing of projects under contracts or grants from the federal government are under more or less constant negotiation between the universities and the governmental agencies concerned, all of which are bound by certain provisions of the appropriation acts and by administrative rulings of the U.S. Bureau of the Budget. In general, the government pays for all materials and personal services used in the project, plus the added overhead costs that are incurred by the institution in the execution of the contract project. Obviously the calculation of these latter costs is no easy matter and is not to be equitably disposed of by any rigid and unchanging formula.

Some of the federal appropriation acts fix a maximum for these payments in the form of a specified percentage (in some instances as low as 15 per cent) of the direct costs. As a consequence, universities in many cases complain that acceptance of the contracts causes them to lose money. There are some indications that the terms may be liberalized.

Another criticism of the total program is that hardly more than a handful of large universities (with disproportionate number of private institutions) receive the bulk of the money. It can be argued that this is inevitable because these are the institutions which have the large research capacities. There is, however, a perceptible tendency toward wider distribution, and the National Science Foundation has begun to operate a program of small grants to small colleges—evidently for the sake of encouraging and strengthening the spirit of research in such institutions.

Federally sponsored research has also been accused of leaning too much toward the applied or developmental stages rather than to the pure or theoretical research which is appropriate in universities and without which progress would eventually cease or be greatly retarded. It has been accused of stressing the physical and biological sciences, to the neglect of the humanities and the social sciences. (The federal government is said to be financing 90 per cent of all university research in the sciences, but only 25 per cent in the social

[5] The subject is treated in depth and detail in Charles V. Kidd's *American Universities and Federal Research* (Cambridge, Mass.: Belknap Press of Harvard University Press, 1959).

sciences.) This adds up to a fear, expressed by some, that the program will divert the universities from their true purposes and destroy or at least distort their institutional integrity.

These misgivings, though sincere, are probably not of sufficient weight to split the partnership that is growing between the universities and the federal government. The policies of the federal agencies seem to be not without some flexibility, and changes are possible when features are perceived to be unpalatable to the universities or to constitute a threat to their necessary independence in the management of their own total programs. Though much of the federal money is granted on the theory of a "purchase of services," nevertheless it is in effect a substantial increase of income for the institutions concerned and is already an element of importance in the total picture of the financing of higher education.

Relations with federal agencies. For the negotiations necessitated by the complexities of the foregoing programs, university presidents often delegate a vice-president or dean familiar with the types of work involved, who is in turn aided by a university business officer and perhaps by a university attorney.

As aids in group representation in Washington, the state universities have the State Universities Association and the land-grant institutions have the large and long-standing Association of State Universities and Land-Grant Colleges, both of which maintain offices with small staffs in the capital. The American Council on Education, which is an association of more than 1000 colleges, universities, school systems, and professional societies, has an active committee on relations with the federal government. Often all three of these organizations[6] join in presenting testimony at hearings before federal administrative agencies or Congressional committees. These may be concerned from time to time with research contracts, with military training units on the campus, with new or old legislation or rulings affecting the federal aids to land-grant colleges, with the status of college and university students under the Selective Service Act, or with a great variety of other matters.

Of recent interest have been the programs of the National Science Foundation providing fellowships for graduate students in designated fields and various institutes for teachers, intended to upgrade

[6] All three have their offices at 1785 Massachusetts Avenue, N.W., Washington 6, D.C.

the teaching of science in secondary schools. The National Defense Education Act of 1958 established somewhat similar and larger programs and added efforts to improve and expand the teaching of foreign languages and of language and area studies as well as vocational education and educational and vocational counseling. Grants for all these features are administered by the Office of Education in the U.S. Department of Health, Education, and Welfare.

It is noteworthy that in almost all of these numerous and important relations with colleges and universities, the federal government bypasses the state governments and deals directly with the institutions. This is a tacit if not explicit recognition of the great importance of higher education to the security and prosperity of the nation. Even though it runs counter to earlier concepts of state sovereignty, it is amply justified on grounds of expediency and, indeed, of necessity. The delays involved in obtaining the assent and cooperation of all the state governments to every innovation in this field would be fatal. Furthermore, an institution of higher education, in its capacity as a corporation, certainly has obligations to the federal government as well as to the state.

As to the future of the relations between the federal government and the states with regard to higher education, a good deal of wisdom is in the words of William Anderson, a distinguished professor of political science at the University of Minnesota:

> I think the course of American history confirms what the practical necessities require, that if the states do not perform such functions adequately, the national authorities, charged with responsibility for the nation's welfare and security, can, must, and will find ways to assist and encourage the states to perform their duties, or even to bypass them if necessary by taking national measures to provide the services required.[7]

[7] William Anderson, *A University Professor Looks at Higher Education in Minnesota* (Minneapolis: Governor's Committee on Higher Education, 1957), p. 3.

CHAPTER IV

Issues Regarding the Sources of Support

Preceding chapters have examined the principal sources of income for colleges and universities. With respect to each of these, there are questions and unresolved issues of some importance, relating to their ultimate social and educational effects in the society of today and of tomorrow.

Perhaps it should be said at first that the virtually certain doubling of enrollments in higher education by 1970 to 1975 raises a strong presumption that income from all the present sources should be maintained and increased as rapidly as possible. It is not difficult to concur with the general estimate that annual operating expenses, to say nothing of capital outlays, will have to be tripled within ten to twelve years. A closer look at some of the social implications, however, may well indicate that the flow of income from some of the sources can and should be increased at rates much more rapid than that from some others. Indeed, the input from some sources should perhaps not be increased at a headlong rate, but eventually decreased or eliminated altogether, heretical as that may seem!

Does dependence upon private philanthropy almost automatically make the donors, especially the large donors, unduly influential in the educational enterprise, thus endangering academic freedom? Does reliance upon tax support surely subject the enterprise to political influences which may likewise strangle its integrity and debase its quality? Can the people of the nation afford to pay for a major part of the enterprise by taxation?

What proportion of the college-age population should be enrolled in formal higher education at the junior college level? At the senior college level? At the graduate and professional level? What part of the cost of operating the enterprise should the students or their families be required to pay as fees for tuition and other services? Let us assume that the answer is different for private and public institutions. Should public higher education be tuition-free?

What are the merits and disadvantages of student aids such as scholarships, fellowships, student loans, and part-time employment? Can the states afford to continue to be the largest single source of funds for higher education? Should the states regiment the state universities and colleges into a bureaucratic system under tight fiscal controls? Should the national government increase its financial partnership with the states and the institutions in the support of higher education? If so, by what means and methods?

These questions have social and political overtones, but they are essential issues in the financing and economics of higher education today. The people are obliged to study them and to answer them as best they can.

The Future of Private Philanthropy

The condition of private giving to colleges and universities was neatly epitomized in the title of one of the small publications of the Council for Financial Aid to Higher Education only a few years ago: *The Trend Is Upward!* The flow of income from private sources —foundations, business corporations, individuals, religious organizations, alumni—is increasing year by year.

A respected economist, Professor Seymour E. Harris of Harvard University, estimates that today's total of approximately $1 billion a year may rise to $1.5 billion by 1970. Some are more optimistic, and guess that the flow will reach $2 billion a year. Even if this should occur, however, the rate of increase will not be keeping pace with the approximate *tripling* of annual operating expenses expected to occur within the same period.

The rather generous tax advantages provided to encourage private giving by individuals and corporations under the federal and state income, estate, and inheritance tax laws will undoubtedly be continued, and perhaps further liberalized. An element of uncertainty is always present, however, because it becomes necessary from time to time to close a conspicuous loophole ingeniously rooted out by indefatigable lawyers.

At the same time, it is manifest that the exemptions allowed by the laws have never been fully taken advantage of by possible donors. This offers ample leeway for expansion.

Giving by business corporations is probably in its infancy. If a few hundred of the larger firms were to donate as much as 1 per cent of their net incomes before taxes each year, the input to colleges and universities would be many times what it has ever been. Alumni giving also grows and will continue to grow, as more and more institutions slowly accumulate longer histories, more graduates and former students, and better organized annual campaigns for alumni contributions.

In private philanthropy the trend is unquestionably upward; and welcome as this information is, the best guess is that the rate of rise will have to be outpaced by faster gains in income from other sources. A highly controversial issue remains: Which other sources?

High Fees or Public Support?

Professor Harris has his own answer to this question. Of the additional $6 billion a year that will be needed for operating expenses by 1970, he wants $2.9 billion—or nearly half—to come from increased student fees. He thinks $1.6 billion can come from economies resulting from the doubling of volume. He thinks only an additional $.5 billion is likely to come from private philanthropy, and $1 billion from governmental sources. He recommends that private institutions raise their fees much nearer to actual cost of the education provided, and that public institutions raise their fees to at least 40 per cent of the cost.[1] This would, of course, mean a doubling of fees for public institutions. This proposal is anathema to the leading representatives of state universities, including the Association of State Universities and Land-Grant Colleges and the State Universities Association. The executive committees of these two associations recently issued a joint statement:

> The process of making students pay an increasing proportion of the costs of higher education will, if continued, be disastrous to American society and to American national strength.
>
> It is based on the theory that higher education benefits only the individual and that he should therefore pay immediately and directly for its cost—through borrowing if necessary . . .
>
> This is a false theory. Its adoption . . . will jeopardize seriously our national strength, reduce our standard of living, and

---

[1] Seymour E. Harris, "College Salaries, Financing of Higher Education, and Management of Institutions of Higher Learning," *American Association of University Professors Bulletin,* 44 (Autumn, 1958), 589–95.

> reverse the entire tradition of equal opportunity in life for your young people.
>
> The primary beneficiary of higher education is society. It is true that great economic and other benefits do accrue to the individual, and it is the responsibility of the individual to help pay for the education of others on this account—through taxation and through voluntary support of colleges and universities, in accordance with the benefits received.
>
> But even from the narrowest of economic standpoints a general responsibility rests on society to finance higher education. The businessman who has things to sell is a beneficiary whether he attends college or not, or whether his children do or not. Higher productivity and higher incomes make better customers for business.
>
> Are we now to abandon the principle of social responsibility for higher education which has put us and kept us at least relatively ahead, turn back the calendar a century or more, make the amount of money the individual has or is willing to borrow the sole determinant of our supply of trained scientists—for example? This is what the extremists (and there are many of them) are proposing.
>
> Since there is little correlation between the intellectual ability of the student and his family income, the American public college or university must not become a device to reverse our historic trend away from a class society. We should continue to open wider doors of opportunity for students of genuine ability without regard to income status.[2]

The statement also asserted the manifest fact that an adequate scholarship system to accompany a high fee structure would require vast sums of money plus a fantastic amount of administrative machinery. It may also be added that it would involve invasions of individual and family privacy that would deter many competent persons from seeking its benefits.

The state universities of the Middle and Far West were founded as keystones of the state educational systems and intended to be free of tuition. The best way to make high-quality higher education as widespread as possible is to offer it without fees or at low cost.

This does not mean that private institutions ought not to raise their fees when necessary. Traditionally they have wide latitude in the management of their own affairs, and it is for them to decide what their fees shall be and what scholarships they shall offer. But

---

[2] Release issued November 13, 1958 by Allan W. Ostar, Director, Joint Office of Institutional Research of the State Universities Association and the American Association of Land-Grant Colleges and State Universities, Washington, D.C.

it is not for them to dictate the fee and scholarship policies of the public institutions. This is no cause for quarrel between private and public institutions. There will be more students than either or both types of institutions can accommodate, and competition in an "economy of scarcity" of students will not be what it once was. Both types of institutions will grow; each will have its own peculiar role and distinctive functions. It is true that considerations of finance as well as numerous other factors indicate that the public institutions will grow more rapidly than the private ones. This will not be the result of any decision by educators, but of determinations by legislators and the general public.

This will mean a large increase in the support of higher education from public funds. The $1 billion of additional annual funds suggested by Professor Harris will be picayunish. It would have to be closer to $3 billion instead. Local districts will be the primary source of support of public junior colleges and municipal universities. States will double their support of state universities and colleges, as well as state aid to local public schools and junior colleges. This will be accomplished by improvement of state tax systems, which is a continual process, and by a restoration of higher education as a public function of unequaled importance, meriting at least 10 per cent of the average state's annual expenditures instead of the 4 or 5 per cent it is now getting.

Furthermore, there is no longer any doubt that higher education is of paramount significance to national survival and national welfare, so that the increasing participation of the federal government in its support will inevitably be enlarged, and the states will not be expected to provide for it wholly from their own tax resources.

Fees are automatically discriminatory against women. Although girls are more numerous than boys in the upper half of high school graduating classes, only about one third of the total of college students are girls. Fewer than one eighth of the total of Ph.D. degrees conferred annually go to women. The percentages of women students in the professional schools (with the exception of schools of nursing, teaching, and social work) are so small as to be practically negligible. This condition is not the result of any absence of ability among young women. Instead it is the product of a melange of social traditions which dictate that woman's place is in the home, that a woman's horizon should be bounded by *Kirche, kinder,* *und kuchen;* and of urges—biological and social—which lead many young women to marry and undertake family responsibilities in their late 'teens and early twenties. Financial barriers also play a large role. In families of low or moderate income having both boys and girls, it is often decided that the meager funds available for college will be used to afford necessary assistance to the boys, not the girls.

The mores are subject to modification and evolution. If the manpower of the nation is to be developed to the maximum, this will involve getting more girls into college and more women into the professions and scientific pursuits at all levels. Women are known to be an essential factor in the phenomenal technological progress of the Soviet Union, where they constitute 51 per cent of all university-level students, 69 per cent of all medical students, 44 per cent of all agricultural science students, and 39 per cent of all engineering students. Thirty-five per cent of all university-level teachers are women. Women students pursue the same courses as men, and there is none of the archaic idea of segregating young women in finishing schools to study such subjects as personal grooming, ballroom dancing, flower arrangement, and the like.[3]

It would not be wise to urge Americans to copy Soviet customs, but social trends have a way of disregarding national boundaries. Who could be unaware that for a century the strong trend toward recognition of women as human beings rather than fragile creatures to be confined on pedestals has progressed a long way in the United States? The implication for finance in higher education is that there will probably be an increasing proportion of women in colleges and universities, and this element may cause aggregate enrollments to rise even faster than the population factors already mentioned would indicate.

Another implication is that since women students are somewhat less able than men to continue in college under financial hardships, and are also for obvious reasons somewhat less willing to borrow money for that purpose, any rise in college fees is in fact discriminatory against women and tends to reduce their proportionate numbers in student bodies. This may well be one of the principal reasons

---

[3] *Report on Higher Education in the Soviet Union,* by a delegation of American University Presidents (Pittsburgh: University of Pittsburgh Press, 1958), p. 32.

why the proportion of women in American colleges and universities is now scarcely greater than it was in 1940.

The Rationale of Student Aids

When it is pointed out that high fees will bar many able young people from college and reduce the output of optimum-educated manpower, the response is that scholarships, fellowships, and student loans can be provided in sufficient volume to impecunious but college-worthy young people. This assurance should not be accepted at face value. For example, it is usually insisted that state systems of scholarships (as in New York, California, and a few other states) or any proposed nationwide scheme of scholarships payable out of public funds shall allow the recipients to attend any reputable institution of their choice. This freedom of option has an attractive aspect, but in fact it turns out that the bulk of the beneficiaries choose high-prestige, high-fee colleges or universities, so that the scholarships become actually indirect subsidies to private institutions. It seems that scholarship holders, chosen on a highly competitive basis, are quite likely to be persons who would have attended college anyway. The scholarship merely enables them to attend a high-fee college, thus having relatively little effect in getting able people into college who would not otherwise be there. Thus the main thrust of the program for the use of public funds may be toward a mere reshuffling of students and indirect subsidies into the high-fee private colleges, rather than toward encouraging additional able students, who would otherwise be deprived of a college education, to attend low-fee or tuition-free institutions of good quality.

This latter characteristic appears to dominate in New York State's recently inaugurated "scholar incentive program," which is on so broad a scale that 80 per cent or more of the annual crop of high school graduates can qualify for payments of from $100 to $300 per year (depending on the economic status of their families) for attendance at colleges charging tuition fees of $200 or more per year. Note that this excludes the tuition-free muncipal colleges in the city of New York and some of the low-fee state colleges which are components of the State University of New York. Little attempt seems to be made to mask the subsidy for, to obviate uncertainties in transfer from the student to his college, the payments of state tax funds are mailed directly to the institutions, not to the students.

Subsidies of this kind have chain-reaction effects. They enable high-fee private colleges to raise their fees without losing students. This in turn tends to strengthen the pressure upon low-fee public institutions to raise their fees also.[4] The long-term net result may be an actual narrowing of opportunity for thousands of competent young people who do not rank in the extremely high percentiles required for Board of Regents' scholarships.

The foregoing is not to be taken as a conclusive argument against scholarships or public aid to private institutions. It seems to suggest, however, that possibly neither nor both of these policies is a complete solution to the problem of broadening higher educational opportunity and of developing the nation's resources of brainpower. It is the maintenance and expansion of low-fee or tuition-free public institutions that may be the principal method of achieving these desirable ends. The principle of public support of public institutions may be more attractive as well as more efficient than that of grants to selected students, but there is a place for both.

National systems of graduate fellowships. In addition to the programs of National Science Foundation Fellowships and the National Defense Education Act Fellowships (see p. 73), the Atomic Energy Commission and the National Institutes of Health also operate substantial systems of subsidizing selected graduate and postdoctoral students. These four programs were reported to enroll a total of about 6600 full-time predoctoral students in 1960–61, not counting postdoctoral students and some categories of "trainees," some of whom were actually graduate students.[5]

These 6600 are all presumed to be serious qualified doctoral candidates, thus distinguished from the large majority of graduate students who have no firm expectations of going beyond the master's degree. It is impossible for anyone to know the precise number of "serious qualified doctoral candidates" in all the graduate schools at a given time, but if it be estimated at a low figure of 50,000, it

[4] In January, 1963, the Board of Trustees of the State University of New York voted to exact minimum tuition fees of $400 a year at all units under its control, beginning in September, 1963.

[5] The National Aeronautics and Space Administration is developing a program of fellowships, on a scale expected to be substantial but not yet precisely determined.

appears that those aided by the national fellowship programs are as yet only a small minority.

At this point it is apposite to note that it was estimated that 40,000 graduate students were employed as research assistants on federally sponsored research projects in universities for 1961–62. These were practically all in the natural science and engineering fields, and many of them were below the master's level. The fact that some large universities are experiencing difficulty in persuading a sufficient number of superior graduate students to accept employment as part-time teaching assistants tends to indicate that the best students apparently often prefer fellowships or research assistantships because these are offered better pay or better opportunities to progress with their individual graduate programs, not that graduate schools are approaching saturation with fellowships and research assistantships in sciences and engineering.

The national fellowship systems are exclusively or largely for the education of scientists in mathematics, physics, medicine, biology, engineering, and other sciences. The program under the National Defense Education Act of 1958 is, however, open to students in the humanities, education, and the social sciences; in 1960–61, 64 per cent of the current fellowships were in those three fields. The purpose of the program is to stimulate the development of new or expanded programs of graduate study approved by the Office of Education upon the application of particular educational institutions. It is intended that the program will "substantially further the objective of increasing the facilities available in the nation for the graduate training of college and university teachers and of promoting a wider geographical distribution of such facilities." It carries provision for payment to the institution of an amount not to exceed $2500 a year to reimburse it for the operating cost of the graduate program "attributable to each fellowship student."

A number of changes in the Act, such as would establish a flat sum for reimbursement of the institution, open the program to doctoral candidates having only one year of graduate work to complete, and extend it to existing programs of study as well as to new or expanded ones, were offered in 1961. Though apparently not specifically opposed in Congress, these changes were not included in the enacted measure which extended the Act for two years and authorized the awarding of 1500 three-year fellowships a year.

The stipends, averaging about $2200 a year (plus allowances for dependents), are intended to cover modest living expenses. Markedly different in design and effect from conventional undergraduate scholarship plans, the national fellowship programs bid fair, if judiciously developed, to add rapidly to the national facilities for graduate study and to the annual increase in Ph.D. degrees in all major fields.

Student loans. It is only with explicit initial qualification that student loans can be discussed at all under the heading of "student aids." A loan is not an aid, except in circumstances under which the funds would otherwise be unobtainable, or obtainable only on less favorable terms as to interest and method of repayment no less favorable. A loan, even when on markedly favorable terms, may in fact turn out to be a grievous detriment in individual cases. If the borrower meets with misfortune (which may take any one of a thousand forms), he and his guarantors or his estate have no protection other than such provisions for leniency in hardship cases as may be incorporated in the particular loan plan, or accompanying insurance provisions.

There is a difference between borrowing for educational expenses and borrowing for the purchase of real property or durable goods. The lending agency cannot repossess the "goods" in which the student has invested the loan funds. This has apparently been overlooked by some persons who have argued vehemently that the volume of borrowing for the purchase of tangible property is enormous, and that borrowing for education would be an equally desirable or even more desirable practice.

It is true that the past experience of colleges and universities operating loan funds of their own has indicated that college students are in general a good credit risk; but the volume has been comparatively very small, and the impression has been strong that students are reluctant to borrow and thus mortgage their futures for current expenses. Especially has this been true of women, many of whom expect to marry and become housewives, and who are likely to be appalled by the idea of approaching marriage with a "negative" dowry in the form of a substantial debt.

Under the National Defense Education Act student loan program, loans up to $1000 a year for a maximum of $5000 are possible. Either undergraduates or graduate students may qualify. Ninety per cent of the funds are supplied by the federal government and 10 per cent by the college or university administering the program. About 2000 institutions, including junior colleges, are eligible. About two thirds of these are actually participating in the program. Some do not because the amounts which could be allotted to them would be too small to justify the paperwork involved; some because they refuse to ask their students to sign the disclaimer affidavit which was required until recently; and some apparently because they are lukewarm or opposed to the principle of the loan plan.

By mid-1960 the fund approximated $79 million, and about 140,000 loans—averaging somewhat less than $500 each—had been negotiated. Women students, who constitute roughly 38–40 per cent of the student body, made up about one third of the borrowers. This fact would be distinctly surprising if one were not aware of the provisions stipulating that (1) "special consideration shall be given to students with a superior academic background who express a desire to teach in elementary and secondary schools" as well as to those having evidence of superior capacity or preparation in science, mathematics, engineering, or a modern foreign language; and that (2) up to 50 per cent of the loan, plus interest, shall be cancelled for service as a public elementary or secondary school teacher, at the rate of 10 per cent per complete academic year of such service. Elementary and secondary school teachers, as a total group, are predominantly women; and it is well known that aptitude and achievement in languages is considerably more common among girls than boys.

To a student reasonably certain of becoming a teacher, the second provision seems virtually to bribe the individual to take half the amount required in the form of a loan in order to get the other half as an outright gift. In other words, it is in effect a half-and-half loan and scholarship plan for prospective public school teachers. This, of course, looks attractive to a financially handicapped girl or boy who is already committed to the teaching profession. But it has its drawbacks and dangers. It places a brake on the student's freedom to change his mind about teaching. It poses a constant danger that the public and state and national legislators will mistakenly regard it as a panacea for the teacher shortage and as a substitute for other necessary measures to make the teaching profession attractive, such as better financing of schools, raising of salaries, and betterment of working conditions.

Presumably, when Congress gives attention to the question of extending the National Defense Education Act beyond mid-1963, amendments will be proposed to modify it in many ways. Among the issues will be the question of whether the student loan provisions should be expanded or whether a scholarship system of appropriate scope should be substituted for them entirely.

Student aids have been discussed because of their inseparable connection with student fees as a source of institutional income. Seemingly no one advocates high student fees without at least giving lip-service to a larger program of student aids. In one strictly technical sense, aids to students are not support of the institution, except in situations where the institution can accept additional students at merely nominal cost to itself—and indeed sorely needs a larger student body in order to operate economically and efficiently—or when the agency financing the student aid not only makes direct payments to the student, but also pays directly to the institution a cost-of-instruction reimbursement for each student.

The Trend Toward Public Support

With the swift expansion of the number and size of the local public two-year community colleges, the current average increase of 20–25 per cent every two years in state appropriations for operating expenses of higher education, and the growth of federal financial participation in various forms, the upward trend in public support is not merely a theory or a form of wishful thinking—it is a fact. Harold W. Stoke is credited with having said, in effect: "Higher education in the United States is now compulsory. It became compulsory when we realized that we cannot survive without it."

All levels of government will continue and expand their parts in this essential enterprise of investing in human capital and refining human resources. Some of the requisite steps, already underway, are: (1) modernization of state revenue systems; (2) enlargement of the federal partnership with the states in continued recognition of the national stake in higher education; and (3) general understanding of higher education as primarily a public function and a public service whose benefits inure largely to society as a whole.

This is not to deny that in an important sense all education is self-education, and that the student must supply the motive. Nor is it to ignore the existence of the view that education is good only if it is acquired at great hardship and that it is primarily a private advantage to the student which enables him to outwit his fellows in the competitions of life, and is therefore not a proper object of tax support. Where two viewpoints are opposed, each citizen has an obligation to choose his own point on the wide spectrum between them and to recognize the trends in either direction.

CHAPTER V

Where the Money Goes: Some Categories of Current Expenditure

Institutional activities are commonly classified under three main rubrics: (1) educational and general, (2) auxiliary enterprises, and (3) student aid. The word "educational" is used here in a rather narrow sense—much more restricted than its accepted connotation in law and in general usage. For example, the courts now uniformly hold that dormitories and dining halls (here classified as auxiliary enterprises) are essential adjuncts of an educational institution and are indeed educational in their purpose and use; and it is, of course, quite obvious that "student aid" is nothing if not educational in purpose. In accountants' language, however, auxiliary enterprises and student aid are set off in separate categories, and for good reason. Auxiliary enterprises are generally expected to be approximately self-supporting, or even profitable, as distinguished from the conventional teacher-and-student classroom and laboratory activities which are not income-producing. Student aid is usually largely derived from restricted gifts which are necessarily handled as separate funds. There is no income except from interest on student loans. Loan funds are in the nature of separate revolving funds.

There is not much point in trying to establish norms for the relative bulk of educational and general activities, auxiliary enterprises, and student aid in the total of current operating expenditures. In a college in which practically all the students live in residence halls and eat in college refectories, this fact alone may make auxiliary enterprises amount to nearly half the total current expense; while in an urban or local district college or junior college, the only facilities of that type may be snack-bars for midday lunch. Again, intercollegiate athletics at some institutions involves a budget of $1 million or more annually; but in many others it is comparatively negligible from a financial standpoint; and in some it is nonexistent.

It appears that in a recent year auxiliary enterprises accounted for about 18.5 per cent of the total current operating expenses of all institutions of higher education in the United States. Student aid expenditures constituted a little over 2.5 per cent. Thus about 79 per cent was for educational and general expenditures.[1]

Auxiliary Enterprises and Student Aid

Before dismissing the two lesser categories at this point, one should notice that within each of them norms can be applied with probably greater precision and better effect than anywhere else in institutional management. For example, the exact cost of meals in a dining hall can be computed with accuracy; and the relationships between price and quality of such commodities as meats, potatoes, and canned apricots can be rather easily ascertained. Hence it is possible to use comparative data and discover reasonably useful standards for the cost of feeding one student for one day or one month in a satisfactory manner. Even here, however, there are many complexities, such as the efficiency of the purchasing process, market fluctuations, and the use of efficient personnel. The competency of dietitians and cooks is important and, in the case of dining-room personnel, differences in costs may depend on whether or not and to what extent students are employed. Such questions will often depend upon the local employment situation.

Here there will be no attempt to go into detail in the matter of comparative standards in the operation of auxiliary activities. Articles on many aspects of the subject have appeared in recent years in the monthly *College and University Business,* and occasionally in other periodicals.

In the field of student aid, interesting figures could be adduced as to the current average stipends carried by fellowships and assistantships in graduate schools, the average pecuniary value of undergraduate scholarships and loans, the proportion of students who receive student aid in some form, and the extent of institutional part-time employment for students. Many related questions, such as the hours, wages, and working conditions of student employees, including part-time instructors and assistants, and the percentages of the total teaching load in different departments which is currently car-

[1] *The Book of the States, 1958–59* (Chicago: Council of State Governments, 1959), p. 278.

ried by teaching fellows, student assistants, and part-time instructors who are students, are also of interest.

There is but little basis on which to establish norms in this area. Data are scarce and there is a tendency toward confusion and controversy. The impact of federal governmental programs necessarily introduces some elements of uniformity, however. The National Youth Administration Student Work Program (1935–41) paid for part-time employment of students at standard rates up to a maximum of $180 in any one academic year, within the limits of the allotments made to each institution. Next came the G.I. Bill for veterans of World War II, and later a similar bill for veterans of the Korean conflict. Under these acts the student received sums for tuition, maintenance, and instructional supplies. The allowances for maintenance were at fixed levels, with some variation to provide for dependents. Since the administration of the acts began in 1945, changes in the value of the dollar have necessitated adjustments of the allowances.

The federal government has also been in the field for a few years with National Science Foundation fellowships, and now comes in on a larger scale with the loan and fellowship titles of the National Defense Education Act of 1958. Loans are not to exceed $1000 per year; total not to exceed $5000. Fellowships carry stipends of $2000, $2200, and $2400 for the first, second, and third years of graduate work respectively (plus $400 a year for each dependent). These figures will have some tendency to be regarded as norms for a time.

Educational and General Activities Other Than Instruction and Research

Costs of instruction commonly constitute from one half to three fifths of the total educational and general expenditures of a college or university.

Departmental research is that which is carried on by personnel who are primarily teachers, for the improvement of instruction within their departments. Its cost, always comparatively small, is usually lumped with the costs of instruction. Organized research, on the other hand, is that which is set up in independent project form, often supported by funds supplied for the purpose by philanthropic foundations, industrial firms, or governmental agencies, through specific grants or contracts. Thus in all studies of costs it is placed in a separate category. A small college may perhaps seldom have any of this type of activity; but in a large university, the aggregate of sums involved in organized research may be so great as to constitute a major factor in the financial picture and thus change somewhat the relationships between instructional and noninstructional activities and the total educational and general costs of the institution.

Some norms of recent years. It will be seen that something by way of norms can be found as to the proportions of total educational and general costs allocated to each of the major noninstructional functions. For example, in a state of relatively sparse population having seven state-supported colleges and universities with an aggregate enrollment of only about 10,000 students, it is reported that for several years about 15 per cent of educational and general costs have been for administration and general expense, 15 per cent for plant operation and maintenance, 6 per cent for library services, and 4 per cent for extension and organized research.[2] This adds up to 40 per cent, leaving 60 per cent for costs of instruction.

In another state having eighteen state-supported institutions of various types, from junior colleges to state university and separate land-grant institution, the proportions turn out to be rather similar. In this instance, instructional costs for each institution are first determined separately, and the norms for the other functions computed as percentages of the instructional cost, as follows: Administration and general expense, 20 per cent; plant operation and maintenance, 27 per cent; libraries, 8 per cent; and departmental research (to be added to instruction), 3 per cent.[3] In Table 5 these figures are translated into percentages of total educational and general expense and compared with the figures for the state previously mentioned.

It is emphasized that although these norms prevail for each of the two states as a whole, they vary considerably among the different institutions according to differences in programs, in emphases on levels of instruction, and in individual needs. It should also be kept

---

[2] *Proceedings of 1954 Conference of Executive Officers of Statewide Coordinating Boards for Higher Education* (Santa Fe, New Mexico. Prepared by James I. Doi, Assistant to the Chancellor, New Mexico Board of Educational Finance), p. 71.

[3] *Ibid.*, p. 69.

in mind that because of differences in accounting practices among institutions, the percentage figures are only approximations and that their exact comparability is always in question.

TABLE 5

PERCENTAGES OF EDUCATIONAL AND GENERAL COSTS DISTRIBUTED TO MAJOR FUNCTIONS IN TWENTY-FIVE STATE-SUPPORTED INSTITUTIONS IN TWO STATES, 1954.

Functions	*State A*	*State B*
(1)	(2)	(3)
Instruction (incl. dept. research)	60%	65%
Administration and general expense	15	13
Plant operation and maintenance	15	17
Libraries	6	5
Extension and organized research	4	0

The Sixty College Study. In independent liberal arts colleges, the costs of the principal functions tend to differ somewhat in proportion, as indicated by a recent analysis of sixty such colleges located in all parts of the country.[4] Here it appears that instruction and research take only about 50 per cent of educational and general expenditures; libraries, 5 per cent; plant operation and maintenance, 16 per cent; organized research, 1 per cent; and that some 28 per cent is expended on administrative and general institutional expenses, classified as general administration, student services, and public services and information. This is no doubt in part the result of the comparatively small size of the institutions, as is illustrated by the fact that among the sixty colleges, general administration alone varies from a median of 10.5 per cent in colleges having enrollments between 200 and 600, to a median of 6 per cent in those having enrollments above 1400. It seems probable, also, that some of the items charged to general institutional expense in these institutions may to some extent be charged to the instructional departments in larger institutions.

Some nationwide statistics. The statistics of all institutions of higher education in the United States for 1953–54 provide another

[4] National Federation of College and University Business Officers' Associations, *A Study of Income and Expenditures in Sixty Colleges, 1953–1954* (Wellesley, Mass.: The Federation, 1955), p. 183; and *The Sixty College Study: A Second Look, 1960,* p. 173 (a repetition of the same study for the year 1957–58, showing no significant changes in the proportionate relationships of the different functions).

set of norms for the relationship of the expenditures for the principal functions to the total of educational and general expenditures. Since extension work plays a much larger role in the operations of some types of institutions than it does in that of others, and since organized research has come to loom large in the programs of many institutions, it is best to look at the distribution of expenses with and without the inclusion of extension work and organized research. This distribution is shown in Table 6.[5]

Column 2 of Table 6 is much more useful as an indicator of norms than is Column 3. Much of the meaning of Column 3 is lost because a majority of the institutions have negligible expenditures for extension and organized research, while for a distinct minority of institutions these items may amount to as much as one third or

TABLE 6

EDUCATIONAL AND GENERAL EXPENDITURES OF ALL HIGHER EDUCATIONAL INSTITUTIONS IN THE UNITED STATES, 1952–53: PERCENTAGES DISTRIBUTED BY MAIN FUNCTIONS

FUNCTIONS	PERCENTAGES *With extension and research excluded*	*Total*
(1)	(2)	(3)
Instruction*	64.20	50.46
Administration and general expense	16.15	12.70
Plant operation and maintenance	15.57	12.23
Libraries	4.08	3.21
Extension and organized research		21.40

* Including departmental research; and including organized activities related to instructional departments.

more of the total. These latter are generally the larger institutions, however, and this fact causes these items to aggregrate more than one fifth of the total of all educational and general expenditures for all institutions.

Faculty Pay: Nonacademic Salaries and Wages

In recent publications of the U.S. Office of Education and the National Education Association, a great deal of detailed data are

[5] Adapted from *The Book of the States, 1958–59* (Chicago: Council of State Governments, 1959), p. 278.

available regarding salaries of college and university teachers, including separate medians and ranges for faculty members of different ranks in varying types of institutions and in differing sections of the country. A relatively uncomplicated sample of such tabulations is shown in Table 7.

Faculty salaries. Salaries of faculty members afford a specics of norms which can be compared with similar data on the earnings of other professional persons such as physicians, engineers, or lawyers, and skilled workers or technicians in various occupations.

TABLE 7

AVERAGE SALARIES OF COLLEGE TEACHERS IN THE UNITED STATES, BY TYPE OF INSTITUTION AND BY ACADEMIC RANK, 1958–59 *

	PUBLIC		PRIVATE	
Year	*College*	*University*	*College*	*University*
(1)	(2)	(3)	(4)	(5)
		Professors		
1958	$8,950	$9,410	$7,030	$10,160
1957	8,520	8,940	6,540	8,860
		Associate Professors		
1958	$7,230	$7,270	$5,880	$ 7,290
1957	6,910	6,980	5,440	6,660
		Assistant Professors		
1958	$6,280	$6,050	$5,080	$ 5,950
1957	6,020	5,850	4,760	5,490
		Instructors		
1958	$5,120	$4,920	$4,410	$ 4,830
1957	4,970	4,780	4,110	4,520

* As reported in the Education Section of *The New York Times* (January 25, 1959).

Such comparisons reveal unmistakably that since World War II faculty salaries have dcclined in relation to the earning of members of the other leading professions and that they have also failed to maintain their former relationship to the wages of skilled and semiskilled workingmen. The narrowing of this latter ratio is perhaps permanent—a result of the grand socioeconomic reorientation of the last thirty years which has produced a permanent reduction of the spread between social classes.

The available norms reveal many points of interest. Teachers of medicine and surgery are paid at much higher levels than teachers of English or history, even in the same university, because as practicing physicians or surgeons their earnings would be very high, and it would be impossible to staff medical schools with competent men at low salaries. Law professors are also highly paid, for similar reasons (but law schools maintain a low ratio of faculty to students, so their unit costs of instruction are not high).

The larger and more renowned universities, either private or public, pay salaries at higher levels and at wider ranges than do smaller institutions. The levels and ranges of salaries are in general somewhat lower and narrower in the southeastern states than in other parts of the country, partly because living costs are lower in a mild climate and partly for historical and other reasons. Public junior college teachers are often enmeshed in the salary schedules of the public school districts to which they belong. These schedules, however, often do not compare unfavorably with salaries paid junior faculty members in large universities. Above the junior college level, and to a considerable extent within that level, college teaching is a highly mobile profession on a national scale, and teachers readily move across the continent, if necessary, to take positions more attractive to them from the viewpoint of salary or other conditions.

Fringe benefits: the security trend. Another social and economic trend having implications for college costs is the so-called social security. Faculty members and employees of every class have now been conditioned to expect numerous fringe benefits of substantial monetary value in addition to their salaries or wages. These include retirement benefits, sick leave, group insurance against the financial hazards of sickness and accident, and the like. All employees are generally covered in the Old Age, Survivors', and Disability Insurance system operated by the federal government, in which specified small percentages of their salaries and wages, up to a maximum of $4800 a year, are deducted as contributions to the system. This is in fact a plan of compulsory saving which reduces slightly the employee's immediately disposable income. The institution is required to make contributions equal to those of the employee. The college incurs at least three new items of cost: (1) pressure to make up the loss of immediate personal income occasioned by deduction of the employee's contribution; (2) the college's own contribution, usually equal to that of the employees; and (3) the additional accounting expense required for computing, withholding, and paying such contributions.

In many of the principal institutions faculty members have for many years had opportunity to place savings in a system of retirement benefits now known as the Teachers' Insurance and Annuity Association. Institutions affiliated with this association make participation compulsory for their permanent faculty members. The individual's contribution is now often as high as 7.5 per cent of his annual salary; the institution's contribution matches it and, in some institutions, exceeds it. This plan is the eventual outgrowth of activities initiated by Andrew Carnegie early in this century. When he created the Carnegie Foundation for the Advancement of Teaching in 1906, his principal aim was to foster the development of well-financed retirement plans for superannuated professors and their wives.

Some state institutions are covered in state teachers' retirement systems. At least some of their employees are often embraced in state employees' retirement systems. Some institutions have institutional retirement systems of their own, unconnected with any of the foregoing systems. Whatever the retirement plan or plans actually in effect, they give rise in greater or lesser degree to the items of additional cost just enumerated. This is also generally true of other social security schemes of the group health insurance type.

Sabbatical leaves. The idea of the sabbatical leave is a college and university tradition much older than the security trend discussed in the foregoing paragraphs. Probably the commonest plan provides for a leave of absence of one year at half-pay, after each six years of service, for permanent faculty members above the lowest rank. There are many variations—some more generous, some less. Experienced commentators say that many professors eligible for sabbatical leave do not take it because they cannot afford the reduction of income.

In theory the sabbatical is for the purpose of enabling the professor to travel and to complete some significant research. From the business standpoint, then, it is good practice to require his application for leave to state where he expects to go and what research plans he intends to execute, and to require that upon the expiration of his leave he shall report what he has accomplished. After all is said and done, however, these requirements would be dictated in any event by good taste and good sense. Since the amount of fresh stimulation the professor has gained, its durability, and the value of the researches he may have completed or moved toward completion can hardly be estimated with precision in pecuniary terms, his reports have no negotiable value and but little consequence in the business office. Presumably the useful outcomes of his leave will be expressed chiefly over several ensuing years in the life and tone of the institution of which he is a part. Meantime the sabbaticals represent a cost to the institution which must be expressed at least in part by dollar signs followed by arabic numerals in the books of account. This is another type of fringe benefit to be added to estimated costs for faculty salaries. It is probably worth, in the long run, a great deal more than it costs; but the costs must be provided for.

Permanent tenure. Now thought to be a general practice, permanent tenure also has financial implications. For example, if desirable flexibility in the application of salary funds is to be preserved, permanency must be withheld from a considerable portion of the faculty—and this is commonly done by requiring a probationary period of two, three, five or more years. This affords a cushion for possible periods of unavoidable retrenchment.

Although tenure is thought to be a general practice, at least two recent decisions of state supreme courts have held that elaborate ordinances of the governing board of a state institution, intended to establish a system of permanent tenure, are of absolutely no legal effect at all when and if the board later decides to dismiss a professor. The most recent of these was in South Dakota, where a professor of agronomy at the state college at Brookings, who had served continuously since 1943, was dismissed by the regents in 1958. This occurred after the regents had conducted an investigation of personnel and administrative affairs at the college and adopted a written report on the subject. The report found that the professor of agronomy had made himself a controversial figure on the campus and had been guilty of insubordination. The best interests of the college and the state required his immediate dismissal, said the report, but his salary should be paid until the end of his current contract year.

The merits of the case were not reviewed in the courts. The tenure ordinance of the board fell because of what was deemed to be a conflict with the statutes of the state. With little apparent effort to conceal his impatience, Judge Hanson of the State Supreme Court, speaking for the unanimous court, said: "The exact meaning and intent of this so-called tenure policy eludes us. Its vaporous objectives, purposes, and procedures are lost in a fog of nebulous verbiage." It was possible to gather from it, said he, that a faculty member of three years' standing or more cannot thereafter be divested unless a complaint is filed against him by the president. He is then entitled to notice and hearing before a seven-member faculty committee, which makes a recommendation to the president, who then decides whether or not to recommend dismissal. If the president decides for dismissal, the accused is then entitled to notice and hearing before the governing board. "Apparently the board could not discharge a member of the faculty with tenure for any reason if the president failed to file a complaint, or failed to recommend dismissal," said the court. "We believe this to be an unlawful abdication of the board's exclusive prerogative and power." The statutes creating the board give it full power to appoint and dismiss the presidents, professors, and all other employees of the institutions under its control; and, in the view of the court, the board cannot divest itself of any of these powers.[6]

It should be remarked that good administrative practice would dictate that dismissal actions should ordinarily be initiated by the president and that a tenure ordinance—even if ineptly drafted and actually ineffective to prevent such an action from being begun by the board—may nevertheless serve as a useful guide to customary procedure. Although the board will not ordinarily take the initiative in such matters, it cannot legally delegate away its power to do so, and therefore it would seem that a tenure ordinance must take account of that fact if it is to be effective.

It should be added that if either the statute of the state or the professor's contract specifies that he shall be removed only for cause, then there is no question but that the board, if it wishes to remove him, must provide notice and hearing on the charges. Its decision,

---

[6] *Worzella* v. *Board of Regents of Education of State* (S.D.), 93 N.W. 2d 411 (1958). A competent critical commentary on this decision is an article by Clark Byse, "Academic Freedom, Tenure, and the Law," in *Harvard Law Review,* 73 (December, 1959), pp. 304–22.

if challenged, will be subject to review in the courts as to the adequacy of the procedure and as to the weight and sufficiency of the evidence.

Enough has been said to indicate that "permanency" is a relative term, and that the principle of permanent tenure will not be as firmly established in state colleges and universities as it is in the public school systems of some states and cities unless and until it is written into the state statutes. In private institutions, the principle—if adopted by the governing board—fares somewhat better because the courts generally hold that a private nonprofit corporation is free to bind itself by contract with its employees in that manner if it so chooses.

Apart from its legal efficacy is the further question of the soundness of the principle of tenure ordinances from the educational and administrative standpoints.[7] Obviously intended to minimize the occurrence of cases of arbitrary injustice and to protect the profession from undue insecurity, it also brings with it undoubted disadvantages which need to be weighed. It militates against the free movement of senior professors from university to university and, together with the tendency of most retirement systems, operates to "freeze" the senior faculty member into his job to mark time under the protection of permanent tenure and in the expectation of retirement benefits. In many cases he is really not happy in his job and it would be a boon to him as well as to his institution if he would seek greener pastures. This is not to deny that many elderly permanent professors retain their enthusiasms and increase their competencies up to the day of their retirement. But not all professors are so fortunate in those respects. Would it be more desirable if every professor had to defend his usefulness and productivity before a jury of his peers every five years?

Under any system, it is always difficult to hold the best ones and get rid of the ones who are merely mediocre and uninspired. Here is the chief implication of faculty administration for financial administration. This is why a president or dean should be free to au-

---

[7] A good affirmative presentation of the case for tenure is the book by Clark Byse and Louis Joughin, *Tenure in American Higher Education: Plans, Practices, and the Law* (Ithaca, N.Y.: Cornell University Press, 1959). See Appendix for the most recent statement of recommended tenure principles and practices, jointly promulgated in 1958 by the American Association of University Professors and the Association of American Colleges.

thorize, subject to the approval of the governing board, an occasional contract calling for a salary far in excess of existing norms, and why it may be a mistake to tie his hands too tightly in the matter of dismissals.

Nonacademic personnel. Colleges and universities necessarily employ substantial numbers of persons for secretarial, clerical, and other office work, skilled craftsmen for maintenance and repair work and for the operation of utility services, truck drivers, groundskeepers, gardeners, and other types of workers. Often the large universities have developed reasonably systematized practices, codified in local administrative regulations, regarding the recruitment, compensation, classification, and working conditions of these employees. Manifestly the management of these functions is increasingly complicated by the recently augmented growth and influence of labor organizations, the development of labor laws relating to collective bargaining, and the increasing volume of fringe benefits.

It is highly questionable that any good purpose is served by covering all or most of these employees by a complicated state personnel system administered from the state capital, as is done by law (so far as the state universities and colleges are concerned) in a considerable number of states. There are many reports of lagging recruiting, misfit classifications, and pathetically comic errors in this long-range control.

Unquestionably many members of faculties spend portions of their time and energies in necessary routine and clerical tasks because of an insufficient supply of clerical assistance. Where this situation exists, it is a false economy and a source of real loss.

CHAPTER VI

Efficiency in Higher Education

The greatest glory of American higher education is its diversity. Its units are not uniform and interchangeable like cogs in a wheel. It is not an assembly-line process. It is craftsmanship and art and indefinable insights which cannot be reduced to a mold.

Ipso facto, there are severe limitations, frustrations, and dangers in attempting to place education on a strict cost-accounting basis in which the production cost of a standard unit is minutely computed. Be warned!

Then why talk of higher education as though it were an industrial operation whose output could be standardized and priced per unit like the output of pig iron or piston rings? Mainly because in a climate where so many things are measured by money, donors and taxpayers often seek evidence that their money is being spent to the best advantage. They want to be assured that educational enterprises are being managed efficiently for the accomplishment of their respective purposes. Reports of the stewardship of their funds are necessary.

In a very real sense, the efficiency of a college or university today cannot be measured until half a century hence, when today's students will have played their roles in life. But the public cannot wait fifty years for a report on which to base this year's decisions.

Thus it has become necessary to adopt, with understanding of their weaknesses and unrealities, some concepts which will serve to denote some standard units of accomplishment. If used with the greatest of caution and if their shortcomings are carefully explained, these concepts may be a means of providing clues to comparative costs among classes, departments, and institutions. These clues may, if accompanied by an adequate comprehension of the differing aims, methods, and settings of the enterprises being compared, afford some useful coloring of the picture needed by a college president who wishes to study the operation of various elements within his own institution in relation to each other or to compare the operation of his own institution with others of similar type, size, and purposes.

It must never be forgotten that this technique, even when refined to the utmost, is always only a crude instrument. For example, the cost of giving one student three credit hours in English Composition may be twice as much in one class as in another, but the results may justify the expense. Filet mignon costs more than hamburger. Moreover, a department of instruction which is overstaffed and clumsily administered may be producing much more for the money than another which is tautly organized.

Unit Costs of Instruction

Measurement and comparison of unit costs can be undertaken in any or all the major educational and general functions of a college, as well as in auxiliary enterprises and student aid. Perhaps the function of plant operation and maintenance lends itself to measurement of unit costs as readily as any function does because the kind and degree of comforts and conveniences derived from plant operation and maintenance are possibly more nearly uniform from building to building and from campus to campus. One must not overlook the fact that it costs considerably more to operate a college plant in a cold climate than in a warm one, and that it may cost more to operate and maintain an old plant or building than a new one. It is also quite obvious that the amount of space to be heated and cleaned is relatively greater per student for shop or laboratory instruction than it is for lecture halls, and that the plant and equipment facilities necessary for instruction and related research increase rapidly as the level of instruction goes upward, so that their maintenance and operation is relatively much more expensive per student for a graduate school than for a junior college.

But this interesting field of plant operation and maintenance is quantitatively less important than the field of instructional service, into which half or more of the institution's educational and general expenditures generally go. Unit costs of instruction have long attracted a good deal of interest, and their computation may be said to have generated, on the whole, more heat than light. Some university presidents, including David D. Henry of Illinois, have openly declared that any computation of unit costs is of very limited use. Says Henry:

> There is no accounting analysis which gives an accurate representation of cost per student. . . . Costs within the institution vary so greatly that an average estimated cost would be meaningless.[1]

It is true that any calculation of unit costs of instruction is only of severely limited value and can cause a great deal of harm if unwisely interpreted. In fact, it means almost nothing of itself, and may acquire some meaning only when thought of in relation to the context from which it is drawn.

First of all, what is meant by "unit"? Conceptions commonly used are (1) the student, (2) the student credit-hour, and (3) the student contact-hour.

What is a student? Some are carrying the normal load of courses that will enable them to obtain a baccalaureate degree in the usual four years or eight semesters. Others may be accelerating their programs by carrying an extra course or two, to permit graduation in less than the normal time. Some may be carrying less than a full program, because of outside employment, or because of health conditions, or for other reasons. Some may be coming only for a course or two each semester while holding a full-time job. Each of these is a student, but a head count of students carrying such differing loads is clearly not an accurate measure of the volume of instructional service rendered. It is necessary to invent a hypothetical unit, the "full-time-equivalent" student, based on the number of credit-hours which is the standard student load in the particular institution. Thus in a four-year, 120-credit-hour course for a bachelor's degree, the full-time-equivalent student is the equivalent of one carrying fifteen credit-hours per semester. The matter becomes somewhat more complex when universities having advanced graduate schools are involved, because at advanced graduate levels the normal student load is often much less than fifteen credit-hours per semester, and in some instances is not measured in credit-hours at all, and hence has to have a credit-hour value more or less arbitrarily assigned to it.

A more minutely refined unit, the student credit-hour itself, may be useful in studies of instructional cost within a single institution,

[1] David D. Henry, "Institutional Cooperation and Coordination in Meeting New Responsibilities," *North Central Association Quarterly*, 32 (April, 1958), pp. 318–24.

where as a rule many students pursue courses in several departments simultaneously.

Measures of cost based on the volume of instruction have to be used with extreme caution in attempting comparisons among institutions, because sensible comparisons can be made only between similar types and levels and areas of instruction. Medical schools, in which a very high-cost program of instruction is not only required by the national accrediting agency but demanded by the importance of the medical profession to the public safety and welfare, cannot sensibly be compared with anything except other and similar medical schools. Here, in crude terms, the annual cost of instruction per student may be $4000 or more, while at the same time in a good liberal arts college it may be less than $1000. When such facts are known, somewhere there must be a decision that such a wide difference in cost is justified. Most kinds of undergraduate engineering and technological instruction, though not as costly as medical instruction, are relatively expensive compared with other undergraduate studies because of a high proportion of shop and laboratory work and expensive equipment.

Moreover, generally speaking, level is as important as type. It has been said that instruction in the senior college or in the upper division in the four-year college costs twice as much as that in the junior college or the lower division, and that graduate work costs at least twice as much as senior college work, so that the ratio among the three levels is about 1–2–4. Actually this is often too low for advanced graduate instruction. Probably a more realistic ratio is 1–3–8.

One reason why advanced undergraduate and graduate instruction are relatively expensive is the proliferation of courses at these levels, and the relatively small numbers of students, in comparison with the lower divisions. This condition prevails at a very large percentage of all four-year colleges and at many universities, but not at a few great universities which severely limit the number of admissions at the freshman and sophomore years but accept many transfer students at the third-, fourth-, and fifth-year levels. These practices will probably be adopted by more of the larger universities, and perhaps also by some four-year colleges, as the wildfire expansion of the two-year community colleges continues. Furthermore, irrespective of these developments, the large universities no longer have—or certainly will not long have—any paucity of students at the senior college and graduate levels. Thus sounder reasons for the costliness of advanced graduate instruction and research are that it requires the leadership of distinguished professors, much man-to-man interchange of ideas between professor and student, and often fantastically costly equipment and apparatus—to say nothing of vast libraries receiving literally thousands of current learned journals from all parts of the world as well as tens of thousands of new books and reports each year.

Taking a dynamic view of the present growth situation in higher education, one can not only observe the foregoing but also conjecture that if the method and spirit of advanced graduate schools could permeate, even slowly and on a limited scale, the four- and five-year institutions, it might tremendously enliven the whole enterprise of higher education and greatly increase the actual learning output.

Distinguishing the levels and types. A great deal of fifth-year work, while possibly more costly than similar types on the senior college level, is not at all comparable to advanced graduate work above the fifth-year level. It would seem that comparisons should be kept within the boundaries of at least four distinct levels of instruction: (1) junior college, (2) senior college, (3) fifth-year, and (4) advanced graduate. Further, it should be confined to comparable types on all levels, so that liberal or general education will be distinguished from the professional and technical schools or departments (even though the latter may be partly general and partly specialized in character).

In considering a group or system of institutions, among which are several two-year institutions, several four-year institutions (some of which offer fifth-year work), and one or more universities (including all these levels and extending upward to the highest peaks of advanced graduate and professional study and research), a minimum of refinement would require that only similar levels and similar professional or technical studies be compared with each other. Thus the data for a university as a whole, in crude form, would never be comparable with those of any other institution—not even with those of another university—because no two universities have precisely the same professional schools, or an identical distribution of professional and technical and liberal arts students, or graduate schools with equal strength and numbers in identical departments.

Indeed, advanced graduate study and research is so much of a risk venture both for the student and the public, and so much of an individual and unique enterprise in each case, that there is very little point in attempting mass comparisons at that level.

In some circumstances high unit costs represent good policy. One other factor needs to be mentioned. A two-year or four-year college may be located in a remote and sparsely populated section of a state, economically undeveloped and without immediate prospects of speedy advancement. Because it does not have the necessary compact demographic base, such an institution may be unable to enroll enough students to bring its unit costs down to anywhere near the level of costs in similar institutions in densely populated and economically favored parts of the state. But young citizens are born and grow up in such unfavored regions. To what extent must the state provide them with accessible educational opportunity, even at double the cost per unit of similar facilities in more favorable locations? This is a question of public policy for the people and their legislators to determine. The matter is cited to demonstrate that very high unit costs of instruction do not necessarily or inevitably mean extravagance or inefficiency or corruption, as is sometimes hastily assumed.

The regrettable fact is that when it is discovered that a college has high unit costs of instruction, that information does not of itself tell whether the institution is being operated wastefully or whether it is being operated efficiently and producing results that fully justify the high cost. However, so practical an authority as the North Central Association of Colleges and Secondary Schools, which has spent decades developing and using techniques for identifying the character and quality of college programs, has for more than twenty years regarded expenditure for educational purposes per student as an important index of institutional quality.[2] And this judgment has been consistently supported by the results of applying to many institutions the numerous other yardsticks the Association uses, as well as the practice of continuing periodic inspections of institutions by teams of competent investigators.

---

[2] John Dale Russell, *The Finance of Higher Education* (Chicago: University of Chicago Press, 1954), p. 152. The original research report on which this policy is based is John Dale Russell and Floyd W. Reeves, *The Evaluation of Higher Institutions,* Volume VII; *Finance* (Chicago: University of Chicago Press, 1935).

Refinement of units. In efforts to fit the unit of measurement more realistically to the operation of the college or university, investigators use smaller units such as the student credit-hour and the student-faculty contact-hour. The former is probably the more practicable of the two, though certainly many conscientious persons will shrilly point out that a credit-hour in Freshman English is not necessarily worth as much as one in Sophomore Physical Education for the same student, nor as much as one in Freshman English for another student. Educators do not deal in standardized units; they only use a sort of fictitious pseudostandard which is known to be vastly variable.

But to use this rubber yardstick is perhaps better than to plead that there is no measuring device. The resulting inaccuracies are in part mitigated wherever large numbers are involved, because of the well-known propensity of statistical data to cluster about a central tendency and to arrange themselves in a normal distribution, in which it is sometimes said that the extreme variants tend to cancel each other out so far as the line of central tendency is concerned. It goes without saying that whenever a variable unit is used as a basis of comparison, it must not be the sole basis but must be used only in conjunction with other appraisal devices which make due provision for the presence and distribution of individual variants.

The student credit-hour is often employed in connection with instructional costs as measured in faculty salary expenditures alone, because salaries constitute the largest element in costs of instruction, and are always on record. Excellence of faculty is the most important available index of excellence of instruction, and since in our modern economy money tends to buy quality, the cost of faculty salaries per student credit-hour is thought to be one of the best available measures of quality in higher education. Obviously such a measure is not infallible in individual cases or with small numbers, but its usefulness increases as the numbers involved increase above the threshold of reliability.

When the student is used as the unit of measurement and the teacher, without reference to his salary, as the unit to be measured, the relationship is expressed as a teacher-student ratio, which is one of the crudest and simplest of norms. Some institutions have maintained that a ratio of 1:10 is necessary for good work. A few assert that 1:20 is sufficient. The current average is probably about 1:13, or perhaps a little higher if junior colleges are included. The subject is complex and lends itself to reliable experimentation only with great difficulty. Consequently there is no really conclusive evidence at the command of those who advocate higher or lower ratios, but it is thought that a rapid increase in the number of students per faculty member would depress the quality of an institution's work.

This does not, of course, preclude reasonable experimentation with large lecture classes, the use of closed-circuit television, or an increase in the amount of independent study done by students. Sometimes, however, these efforts will turn out to be more costly than the methods of instruction they are intended to supplant.

Utilization of Plant Facilities

College classrooms and laboratories are not in use every hour of every working day. Most buildings are in use less than six full days per week. Many stand idle during intersession vacations, and generally there is only light occupancy or complete vacancy for considerable periods during summer months. Available norms indicate that half the institutions use their classrooms an average of twenty-one hours a week or less.[3]

The high cost of construction and maintenance and the continuing increase in numbers of students combine to build up pressure for fuller utilization of existing space. Scheduling of classes at all hours of the day (and evening) can push the norm upward. Evening classes are a necessity for urban institutions seeking to serve students and adults who are obliged to pursue full-time employment. In some institutions the plant is in practically double normal use—from early morning until five to six P.M. it is full of day students, and from six to ten P.M. it teems with evening students.

Changes in the college calendar, such as from the traditional two-semester plan to four equal quarters with only brief pauses between, can mean fuller utilization of plant. Any such shifts may collide with some traditional perquisites or prerogatives of faculty members: some feel abused and oppressed if their classes can not

---

[3] John Dale Russell and James I. Doi, *Manual for Studies of Space Utilization in Colleges and Universities* (Athens, Ohio: American Association of Collegiate Registrars and Admissions Officers, 1957). More recent data assembled by Doi indicate no great change in the median.

all be scheduled at ten or eleven o'clock in the forenoon, and others are averse to contemplating the disappearance of the long summer vacation. In fact, however, year-round operation of the college can preserve this long-accustomed perquisite of the profession. College teachers can be given leaves of absence during any quarter of a four-quarter year, and often the particular quarter can be at their own choice.

Studies of space utilization also often include facilities other than classrooms and laboratories. Offices for faculty members and clerical employees, as well as space for administrative offices, come under scrutiny. And it is here that a literal-minded efficiency expert, ignorant of the academic situation may unwittingly kill a cow by shooting at a gnat. Imagine the case of the productive professor who has only five years to go until retirement and who has for decades occupied, with his secretary, an oversize room lined with books from floor to ceiling. In the center of the room is a large table where he conducts small seminars and occasional conferences with students and other faculty members. In this room an international scientific journal is edited and many other scholarly papers prepared.

After measuring the square footage, the expert in space utilization reports that it is greatly in excess of normal requirements, and recommends that the elderly secretary be moved to a stenographic pool, perhaps in another building, that the professor be moved to a cubicle of standard size, or that the desks of three junior faculty members be moved into his office. If this recommendation is followed, the unhappy reverberations will resound for at least five years, and the loss to the institution will far exceed any possible gains from this more "efficient" space utilization. This is what wise presidents and business managers mean when they say that sometimes sacred cows produce great quantities of good milk.

Efficient Management of Investments

In what proportions should an institution's endowment be invested in real property, government bonds, municipal bonds, utility bonds and debentures, industrial stocks, and other securities? What constitutes a good distribution of common stock holdings, as among rails, industrials, commercials, and other types? One way of obtaining a partial basis for judgment on such questions as these is by keeping informed as to the current practice of other similar institutions in these respects.

Scarcely more than a generation ago, common stocks were generally not regarded as appropriate investments for charitable trusts. They were said to be speculative; and whereas a prudent man in the management of his own money might hazard the risks in the hope of growing rich, a prudent trustee of charitable funds would adhere to a higher regard for safety. Now, however, it is everywhere recognized that common stocks, if wisely selected, not only produce a higher rate of return than most other investments but are also an excellent hedge against inflation because they appreciate in value during upward swings in the business cycle. Inflation cuts the value of the dollar invested in bonds as well as the dollar received as a fixed return, but it has the opposite effect in the case of common stocks. Real estate, too, is a hedge against inflation, but it has its own peculiar disadvantages as a form of investment for a charitable corporation. The upshot is that endowment investments should be diversified, but the proportions of different types in the portfolio must change somewhat from time to time according to prevailing and prospective economic conditions. Here, as everywhere, the prevailing norms have a certain usefulness—but they are never a substitute for judgment.

This is illustrated by the report that in 1957–58 the University of Chicago was able to obtain a return of slightly more than 6 per cent on its invested funds. The average small private college, however, almost certainly got no more than 4 per cent on its endowment for the same year. The difference is accounted for by the expertise in the investment field which a large fund can justifiably employ.

Formulas as Guides in the Allocation of Funds to Groups of Similar Institutions

> The work of the universities does not lend itself to regulation and direction by an external authority. . . . The drive for uniformity, which so often follows extension of State activity, is due very largely to considerations of administrative convenience and economy which are not very relevant or important in the field of university development.

The quotation is not from an American state university president annoyed by fiscal controls emanating from the statehouse. It is from a 1948 report of Nuffield College of Oxford University entitled "The Problem Facing the British Universities."[4]

Wherever a state is confronted with the problem of allocating financial aid or support to several institutions of higher education, tension becomes acute and an easy way out is sought by the responsible authority. In the United States, the competing claims were traditionally put forward in a battle of pressures in state legislative committee-rooms, and finally settled during the hectic last days of limited legislative sessions. Then came the executive budget system, under which a fiscal deputy of the governor receives and revises the budget requests of all state agencies before they go to the legislature with the governor's recommendation. Concurrently, on a somewhat smaller scale, came a movement toward having all higher educational institution budgets coordinated and consolidated by a permanent lay board. In some cases the board was set up to exercise full operating control over all the institutions; in others it was set up only to exercise a coordinating influence, usually by advisory and persuasive methods, with the institutional governing boards continuing in operating control.

Overlooking many detailed differences, one can say the consolidated operating board now exists in twelve states, and the superimposed fiscal coordinating or advisory board (often of recent origin) functions in a dozen others. Moreover, in several additional states the state colleges (apart from the state university) are likewise jointly governed or fiscally coordinated. At this point the merits and drawbacks of these systems and their relations to the system of statewide executive budget control which operates in every state, although in varied forms will be ignored. Instead, the concern is with the development and use of norms and their combination into formulas to guide the allotment of funds. Four examples are at hand. Only the salient characteristics will be noted here. They are sketched in the past tense because rapid changes occur in the techniques employed, as well as in the normal monetary values involved.

---

[4] Quoted in Dodds, Hacker, and Rogers, *Government Assistance to Universities in Great Britain* (New York: Columbia University Press, 1952), p. 101.

Kentucky. Coordination of preliminary data for the budgets of the five state colleges (excluding the state university) is accomplished by a statutory council of presidents, governing board members and others, which employs a full-time executive officer. The rudimentary formula utilized as an aid recently allotted a "base" faculty of 46 members for the first 800 or fewer students, and one additional member for each additional 27 students. The institution's salary allotment was the product of its number of faculty members multiplied by the average faculty salary for the five institutions ($6200 for 1958–59). To the salary allotment was added 20 per cent for other instructional expenses.

The basic library allotment was $25 per student (the minimum standard of the Southern Association of Colleges and Secondary Schools).

Administration and general costs were allocated to nine separate subcategories; operation of the training school for practice teaching was treated as a distinct enterprise. (This is in the nature of an organized activity in connection with instructional departments, comparable to teaching hospitals and agricultural college farms connected with university schools of medicine and agriculture.)

Plant operation and maintenance and special costs were the two remaining major categories. For all categories other than instructional expense and libraries, the basis was current practice, plus consideration of relative size of the institutions, enrollment trends, new facilities added, and adequacy of current practice.

Probable income from sources other than state appropriations was computed and deducted from the estimated expenditure requirements to determine the recommended state appropriations.

Oklahoma. Having eighteen state institutions of diverse types and sizes, Oklahoma divided them in three categories:

1. Junior colleges ("base" faculty of 29 for any enrollment less than 500; one added per 40 students over 500).
2. Four-year colleges (59 teachers up to 1000 students, plus one per 30 from 1000 to 1500, and one per 25 over 1500).
3. Major universities (453 teachers up to 6800, plus one per 25 over 6800).

Average salaries currently effective for the respective types were $4600, $5200, and $6000 for nine months, with 2/9 added for summer work for one half of regular faculty in six selected institutions, and for one third of regular faculty in all other institutions.

For other instructional costs, 25 per cent was added.

To the total thus accumulated, the following percentages were added:

Administration and general expense	18%
Research (departmental)	3%
Extension and public service	10%
Library	8%
Plant operation and maintenance	27%

The total thus accrued, unless modified, was the recommended appropriation, less from 10–25 per cent to be derived from fees and other local institutional sources.

Entirely separate formulas, roughly similar to the foregoing, were used for seven units: schools of medicine and veterinary medicine, a technical branch of one university, university hospitals, state geological survey service, agricultural experiment station, and agricultural extension service.[5]

Texas. Here the formula for determining average teaching salaries was based on separate monetary valuations per student semester credit hour in sixteen types and fields of instruction, and differentiated for three levels: undergraduate, master's (fifth year), and doctoral (sixth and seventh years). Among the lowest were liberal arts at $10.18, $23.33, and $66.67 for the three levels respectively, and library science (not offered on the third level) at $10.37 and $29.70. Law, regarded as equivalent to the second level, was computed at $14.67, while social service (offered only on the second level) was set at $42.22. Veterinary medicine, rated as in part equivalent to the second level and in part to the third, was $23.33 and $80.00 respectively. Among the highest valuations were $95.83 for doctoral-level engineering or science, and $86.67 for doctoral-level fine arts or business administration.

The norms for administration, libraries, and plant operation and maintenance cannot be detailed here.

California. Here, as in Kentucky, efforts of this nature were applied only to the state colleges (of which there were then nine), and not to the state university; and apparently were confined to a staffing formula. This had developed over a period of some eight

[5] Adapted from *Eighth Biennial Report of Oklahoma State Regents for Higher Education* (Oklahoma City, Okla.: The Board, 1956), pp. 74–78.

years, largely by a committee consisting of the deans of instruction in the nine colleges under the chairmanship of the specialist in curricula of the Division of State Colleges in the state department of education. The initiative came from the state department of finance in 1949 and 1951. The version of January, 1957, was kept in use at least up to the end of 1958.[6] It was among the most complex of such instruments. Occupying twelve pages in its most compact skeletal form, it cannot be detailed here. In brief, it classified all courses offered into six categories according to the amount of time required of the instructor for each hour of student credit. Within each of the six major breakdowns there was further minute subdividing of the instructor's activities adjudged appropriate for each course, so as to exhibit what constituted a total work-week of forty-five hours. By applying this to all courses contemplated, in accord with projected enrollments in each course and total projections for the college, it was possible to deduce the number of teachers needed. General practice was not to provide for classes of fewer than ten students in the lower division or fewer than seven in the upper division. There was an elaborate "Table of Breaking Points" indicating the number of students in each type of class which would justify provision for an additional section of that class. These breaking points ranged from as low as ten in a demonstration-laboratory for clinical practice to as high as fifty in ordinary lecture-discussion classes or in bands and choruses. The formula was used solely to determine the number of full-time teaching positions required to staff a college instructional program, as a beginning basis for planning the budget.

The Future of Formulas

The four examples just sketched include two states in which a formula was applied only to state colleges roughly comparable in general type (though they actually varied greatly in size and programs). In one of these states (Kentucky) the formula was relatively simple, largely on a student-enrollment basis. In the other (California) it was much more complex, made so in an effort to account for differences in teaching loads in various types of instruc-

[6] *The Faculty Staffing Formula of the California State Colleges* (January, 1957). Mimeo.

tion and for variations among the total programs of the several institutions.

In two other states, the formula was applied to larger numbers of more diverse institutions, including the state universities and separate land-grant colleges in both states, and the state junior colleges in one. In both instances the formulas were comparatively simple, but differentiated on a basis of the levels of instruction. In Oklahoma the distinction was among junior colleges, four-year colleges, and universities. In other respects the formula was nearly as simple as in Kentucky, except for the exclusion of several schools and divisions to which the blanket formula would obviously not be successfully applicable. In Texas the vertical distinction was made among undergraduate, master's, and doctoral levels; and there was additional substantial differentiation among sixteen fields of instruction on each of the levels, accomplished by assigning a normal monetary cost figure per semester credit-hour in every instance. Though much more varied than either the Kentucky or Oklahoma formulas, the Texas device scarcely approached the complexity of the California formulas.

Are these devices in the nature of straitjackets, born in the minds of economy-cultists bent upon strangling the institutions without regard to educational results? Or do they represent the imperfect beginnings of a technique that will eventually be refined to a point where it will become indispensable to the state and to the institutions alike? Probably no one knows with certainty.

Legislators, taxpayers, and donors sometimes demand to know precisely where their money is going and why. Within reason, they are entitled to know. But how far does the complexity of the computations go, before it becomes a reductio ad absurdum and costs more than it is worth? And is it true that minute inspection of every detail of the internal fiscal management of an institution, and potential interference in the control of every small item by an external noneducational authority spells the doom of the free spirit and high morale which are priceless ingredients of a college or university? Moreover, is it really necessary that legislatures and the public should concern themselves with the details of finance and administration in order to make decisions at the much higher levels with which they must deal?

The province of the legislature. Arthur Naftalin, formerly

Commissioner of Administration for the state of Minnesota, one of the wisest of state fiscal officers, has said:

> I should divide the problem of fiscal control over state-supported higher education into two parts. First there is the initial question of what portion of the state's total economic resources should be devoted to higher education, and second the expenditure and internal allocation of the state support once it has been voted. With respect to the first stage I believe this is wholly, appropriately, and inescapably within the jurisdiction of the governor and the state legislature. This determination is inevitably a political one and, under our constitutional system, must be made with responsiveness to the public will as expressed in our democratic elections.
>
> But with respect to the second stage, once the elected representatives have spoken, fiscal control should become the responsibility of the academy itself, as represented and symbolized by the regents or trustees or college board. It should be their responsibility to determine how the limited resources available shall be distributed among the infinite number of competing academic needs. To impose upon this process the will and direction of state fiscal officers constitutes an encroachment that is potentially extremely dangerous.[7]

The formulas discussed were used only as a basis for budget preparation, it is true, but that process is at the root of control of educational policy. At its lower and more detailed levels it should engage the attention of institutional presidents and governing boards set up for that purpose; but ideally the scrutiny of the public, of legislators, taxpayers, donors, should be focused on broader questions of social policy at higher levels, such as (1) What percentage of the state's gross annual product (or aggregate income from all industries and employments) shall go for education? (2) Of this percentage, what proportions shall go for public elementary and secondary schools, and for higher education, including junior colleges? (3) Of the proportion allotted to higher education, what parts shall go to each of the several state-supported institutions? Below this level, presidents and governing boards should be free to make their own decisions. That is the essence of their particular functions.

It may be a mistake to think that a minutely detailed and immensely complicated combing of current practice is essential as a

[7] Memorandum prepared for the Committee on Government and Higher Education, Baltimore, Md. (September 27, 1957), p. 5. Mimeo.

basis for the high-level decisions. It may instead tend to lead one to prejudge them according to the mold of the past, and to exclude bold and original broad-scale consideration of the major problems involved.

Statistical manipulations, regardless of how refined or sophisticated they may become, will never be a substitute for human judgment. The danger is that they may be easily used as a defense for mediocrity and as a shield for short-sightedness.

The real grist for statewide policy decisions. It may be that the currently popular procedure for formulating high-level decisions is inverted. Instead of plunging into the underbrush and trying to dissect every leaf and place it under the microscope, might it not be better for the state's policymakers to begin by circling the area in a helicopter and inspecting the forest as a whole? Should they preoccupy themselves with such questions as whether an institution's expenditures for lead pencils seem to be slightly in excess of normal, or should they ponder instead such queries as:

1. Shall the state make a suitable type of education beyond high school easily and freely accessible to every high school graduate in the state?
2. What long-run effects would this have upon the security and economy of the state and the nation?
3. Shall the state maintain at least one principal state university, which shall be of unsurpassed excellence and of merited world renown, whose advanced graduate studies and research activities shall maintain a leading position in the swiftly progressing scientific and technological and humane developments of the time?
4. Shall the state actively pursue a policy leading to the location of at least a two-year college, offering liberal and general, technical and occupational education to high school graduates and adults, within commuting distance of the home of every citizen, so far as practicable?
5. Should student fees in state universities and colleges be reduced or abolished, as a means of keeping the doors open to talented youth of both sexes and developing to the optimum point the human resources of the state and the nation?
6. Should the state recognize that enrollments in public universities and colleges must grow more rapidly than those in private institutions, and take appropriate steps to provide augmented financial support in accord with the realities?

These are a few of the great and simple issues which should concern state legislatures and state executive officers. A constant probing into the minutiae of internal college administration will not supply the answers. A broad awareness of the oncoming changes in science, technology, economics, and demography within the state and throughout the world is essential.

Some of the foregoing questions of public policy will receive different answers in different states, according to widely varying conditions and traditions. A nationwide policy continues to take form. It should not be doubted that the most affluent society in history will support higher education on an unprecedented and rapidly expanding scale.

CHAPTER VII

The Sources of Real Waste and Loss

It is a truism that colleges and universities can improve their management. This would be the case even if all their current practices were assumed to be perfect, for changes in conditions outside their control would continually create needs for new policies and methods. The same proposition is true for the states and the nation as corporate units. To say that there will always be a place for better management is not necessarily to cast any aspersions upon the current administration. Evolution is a never-ending continuous process—the persistent pursuit of a goal, not the climactic attainment of a state of perfection once and for all.

In preceding chapters various possibilities of progress have been mentioned, and some of the limitations of their application in institutions of higher education have been discussed. The situation may be summed up in the apt words of Harold W. Stoke, president of Queens College in the University of the City of New York: "If the experts ever succeed in making higher education efficient, it will be more inefficient than it is now! The cost-accounting type of mind will never be happy with higher education."

There is a decidedly higher plane of generality on which issues of overwhelming importance relating to the total role of colleges and universities in human society as a whole—in the nation and in the states—gravely need to be noticed, clarified, and resolved.

Higher education is a means of optimally developing the human resources of the state, the nation, and society. As such, it is clearly a social or public function and responsibility to make sure, so far as is possible, that every individual shall have optimal opportunity to upgrade his latent capacities to their fullest potential. In less high-flown terms, this means that the progress of the whole nation is retarded by any denial of legitimate opportunity to any college-competent high school graduate of either sex for any such reason as racial prejudice, lack of appropriate educational counseling, social snobbery, or lack of money.

A Mainspring of the National Economy

It is too well known to need repetition that all these causes are actually operating to keep thousands of superior young men and women out of college in this country, the most affluent in all the world's history. It follows inevitably that the whole society is denying itself for the next fifty years the talents that are thus lost. The consequences will be a weaker economy, a lower standard of living, a reduction of the chances of national survival, and a lower level of civilization than that which is almost within grasp.

This matter is too important to be left wholly to private generosity or to any pricing system based on orthodox economics. Once the all-pervasiveness of this issue in this latter half of the twentieth century is comprehended, it will be perceived that raising the educational achievement of individuals makes better producers and better consumers, reduces unemployment and speeds economic growth, and creates human capital. Past investments in education are now being credited with much of the nation's gains in industrial productivity over recent decades, utterly impossible though it be to compute this with any precision because of the multifold channels through which the benefits of education flow.

Failure to Develop Talents Is the Nation's Loss

With the swift acceleration of research and discovery that has taken place within a generation and bids fair to continue, the role of higher education cannot but be multiplied in the next generation. The explosion of knowledge and the explosion of population make this inescapable.

It seems almost petty to debate whether or not it is feasible or advisable to build up the annual operating expenses of all higher education from the present slightly less than 1 per cent of the gross national product to perhaps 2 per cent. There is no serious question as to whether this expenditure can be afforded in this affluent society. The debate, such as it is, concerns smaller matters of the nature, for example, of an exactly equitable interchange of students among the different states (so far as the state-supported institutions are concerned). This is of no consequence from a national standpoint, except that it is an argument for added federal support. In these times of mobility of population, any degree of failure in any state is the nation's loss.

Comparisons Among States

To get an idea of the standing of a state in relation to other states, numerous indices may be used, such as total population, total college-age population, value of farm products sold, value added by manufacture, personal income received by residents, federal internal revenue collections, retail sales, national bank assets, life insurance in force, postal receipts, and motor vehicles registered.

With these figures, such items as total expenditures for higher education, total enrollments in higher educational institutions, and totals of degrees granted at three levels can be compared.

If personal income receipts and the total expenditures for higher education are reduced to a per capita basis, the picture is sharpened somewhat. Hungate has recently done some work of this kind, showing that in 1952 there were wide variations among the states as to effort to support higher education, as computed from the relation between per capita personal income and per capita expenditure for higher education.[1] A small glimpse of his findings appears in Table 8.

TABLE 8

RANKING OF SELECTED STATES AS TO EFFORT TO PROVIDE TOTAL CURRENT SUPPORT FOR RESIDENT INSTRUCTION, 1951–52

State (1)	*Per Capita Income* (2)	*Per Capita Support* (3)	*Rank (based on computed "effort")* (4)
Colorado	$1,594	$124.36	1
California	1,950	104.77	19
Louisiana	1,181	64.14	24
Montana	1,714	91.82	25
Michigan	1,789	89.64	30
Pennsylvania	1,699	66.99	48

Most of the states ranking high in effort were some of the less-developed states in the west or southeast, while some ranking low-

[1] Adapted from Thad L. Hungate, *A New Basis for Support of Higher Education* (New York: Columbia University Press, 1957), p. 32.

est were highly industrialized states with high per capita incomes (such as Ohio, which ranked forty-fourth).

Allen and Axt set forth some data showing the position of state-supported higher education in relation to that of other principal state functions, such as highway construction, welfare, health, and public safety, showing that higher education is a comparatively unimportant state burden in terms of dollar expenditures and that federal subsidies for the other functions—which require the states to match the federal funds with money out of their own revenues—have an adverse effect upon state support of higher education. The percentage of the total of state expenditures accounted for by higher education dropped from 10 per cent in 1915 to 4 per cent in 1949.[2] Since then it has risen only slightly.

Adequate data of the kind dealt with by Allen and Axt are somewhat difficult to assemble, and much more work in that area could be done to good advantage.

International Comparisons

Attempts at accurate comparisons of the proportions of the national income spent for higher education by different nations of the world are rarely made. They are, of course, immensely difficult because of differences in the structure and operation of national economies, wide variations in methods of financing higher education, and fluctuations in the values of currencies.

A member of an American mission which traveled to the Soviet Union to observe the educational system declared that "last year the USSR spent about 3 per cent of the gross national product of the country for higher education . . . in contrast to the 1 per cent spent by the United States on all higher education, public and private."[3] He also reports that there are no tuition fees and that 83 per cent of the students receive stipends of 300 to 800 rubles a month, "which is adequate to cover basic living costs." This, of course, goes a long way toward modifying the validity of the comparison with

[2] H. K. Allen and Richard G. Axt, *State Public Finance and State Institutions of Higher Education in the United States* (New York: Columbia University Press, 1952).

[3] Franklin D. Murphy, "Some Comments on Soviet Higher Education," Address to Association of American Colleges, Kansas City, Mo. (January 6, 1959), pp. 4, 5. Mimeographed.

the U.S., where fees are increasing and scholarships are not abundant. If one third of the total Soviet expenditure for higher education goes for stipends, then the apparent ratio of 3:1 as to percentages of the total national incomes is reduced to 2:1.

The same observer also reports many senior professors in the Soviet Union receive salaries six times the pay of a laborer, whereas in the U.S. few professors receive as much as twice a laborer's pay. Soviet professors also get substantial extra pay for writing books, monographs, and research contributions, and for honors such as election to the national academy of sciences. They are allotted housing facilities much superior to those of most other professional workers, and enjoy very high prestige. There is no permanent tenure; each professor must stand for re-election before a body of his peers every five years and defend his usefulness and productivity. Men may retire at sixty and women at fifty-five. The doctoral degree is a credential more difficult to obtain and requires longer study than the American Ph.D., but it is practically prerequisite for a professorship. This gives a slight inkling of some foreign norms that afford interesting comparisons with our own.

Failure to Develop Talents Is the Individual's Loss Also

Although it becomes ever more clear that the trend is strongly toward public responsibility for the financing of higher education, and a school of economists has arisen to point out that augmented public investment in human capital is a present and future need of prime importance, this does not absolve the individual and the family of responsibility. Nor does it relieve the financial pinch afflicting millions of low- and moderate-income families now having one or several children soon to reach college age. In many of these families the bitter choice must be made to help finance the education of brother as against sister, or of younger children as against older, or vice versa.

It may be said that prudent foresight could have provided savings or insurance proceeds for the education of the children of the family; but this, in the face of the facts of life, is largely a species of sophistry. Shortly before or at about the time these children were born, many of their parents were giving up to four years of their lives to wartime military service at nominal pay. Their lives, and those of *their* parents, had been disrupted by the great depression of the 1930's. To be sure, this is no argument against thrift and prudence, nor is it intended as such; but to assume blandly that low- and moderate-income families can readily accumulate resources of a magnitude to match the inflated minimum private costs of higher education is flatly unrealistic. Minimum private outlays now range from $5000 to $10,000 for a four-year course, with exceptions at both ends of the scale. The average outlay for an unmarried student at a state university seems currently to be about $1700 for one academic year. Besides, the student is foregoing the chancc to earn two or three times these sums in full-time remunerative work.

Is all this negated by the bromidic tradition of "working one's way"? Not at all. Years ago James Bryant Conant had the courage to remind the nation that good education is scarcely possible without a modicum of leisure; that the double burden of earning subsistence and doing college work is too much for most young people and often means damaged health and diluted learning, not to mention breakdowns and failures. It is trite to recall the bromide in reverse: "Give college a chance to work its way through the boy." No one could fail to admire and applaud the courage and stamina of those rare persons who have succeeded in completing their formal education against such heavy odds, but this is far short of jumping to the conclusion that what a few have accomplished should be adopted as the standard of practice for all, or that it is by any stretch of the imagination to be thought of as possible for many.

Advice to Today's Students and Their Families

What of the college-competent students and their families who are now faced with the barriers of private financial inadequacy? What shall be their personal strategy in the absence of any sudden speeding-up of the inexorable but slowly moving forces that have been observed?

1. For the first two years beyond high school, choose a public two-year community college within commuting distance from your parental roof, if possible. Select an occupational course if you intend to enter remunerative employment after a year or two. Get into the "college-parallel" course if you are ambitious to extend

your education beyond two years, and demonstrate your ability to make a success of it.

2. If you rank high scholastically in high school, begin to reconnoitre for college not later than your junior year. Try for scholarships. Ask your high school teachers, counselors, and librarians for nationwide directories of available scholarships. The United States Office of Education issues one every two years. Do not be overconfident about a scholarship. Though the number appears large, it is small in relation to the total number of able and needy students. Professor Seymour E. Harris of Harvard University says "any likely scholarship program is not apt to provide aid for more than 25 per cent of the student body. The average student can be helped only through low tuition charges."[4]

3. Use whatever connections you have through family, friends, or teachers to obtain scholarships or reasonable part-time work opportunities at colleges with which they are familiar. You might consider corresponding with one or more of the comparatively few colleges which arrange for their students to alternate periods of a few weeks in the classrooms with equal periods at full-time employment in business, industry, or elsewhere. Thus the time required for a baccalaureate course may be perhaps six calendar years instead of the customary four academic years. This is called higher education on the "cooperative plan" with industry. Your high school counselor or librarian can find for you a list of such colleges.

4. If you have completed two years of college with a good record, and want to continue at some college other than the one you have attended, your chances of finding a welcome and some species of student aid or self-help opportunity are considerably better than they would have been at the beginning of your freshman year. Reexamine the chances.

5. If you have a baccalaureate degree and are ready for graduate work, you might try for a fellowship, available either at the university of your choice out of its own funds, or out of funds provided by one of the national fellowship programs mentioned in this book. (See index.) Your college or university counselors can inform and advise you about this.

6. If you want to finance your college career from loans, regard-

[4] Seymour E. Harris, *Higher Education: Resources and Finance* (New York: McGraw-Hill Book Company, Inc., 1962), p. 202.

less of whether you are a freshman or a graduate student, try for a National Defense Education Act loan at the college of your choice. About two colleges out of three are in this program, but this does not guarantee that all applicants for loans can get them. Some students do not want to undertake a burden of debt, and their families advise against it. But this is for you and your family to decide.

For the sake of brevity, the foregoing statements have been phrased rather bluntly. They are not meant to sound imperative; they are only suggestions for you to consider. The decision in each case is yours. Perhaps none of them appeals to you. But this book is not a manual on "How To Get Into College and Stay There." Its main purpose is to give a broad view of how important higher education is to the individual and to the nation, how colleges get money and spend it, what changes and tendencies are in progress, and some of the things one needs to know in order to think about the past, present, and future of the whole enterprise of higher education, as a citizen responsible for helping to form public policy.

Bibliography

Advancement of Understanding and Support of Higher Education. Report of Conference at White Sulphur Springs, February, 1958. Washington, D.C.: American College Public Relations Association, 1958.

Allen, H. K. and Richard G. Axt, *State Public Finance and State Institutions of Higher Education in the United States.* New York: Columbia University Press, 1952.

American Assembly, *The Federal Government and Higher Education.* Englewood Cliffs, N.J.: Prentice-Hall, Inc., 1960.

Andrews, F. Emerson, *Philanthropic Foundations.* New York: Russell Sage Foundation, 1956.

Annals of the American Academy of Political and Social Science, Vol. 301. Especially pp. 93–210, "Methods of Financing Higher Education." Philadelphia: University of Pennsylvania, The Academy, September, 1955.

Babbidge, Homer D., Jr. and Robert M. Rosenzweig, *The Federal Interest in Higher Education.* New York: McGraw-Hill Book Company, Inc., 1962.

Berdahl, Robert O., *British Universities and the State.* Berkeley and Los Angeles: University of California Press, 1959.

Chambers, M. M., *The Campus and the People.* Danville, Ill.: Interstate Printers and Publishers, Inc., 1960.

———, *Chance and Choice in Higher Education.* Danville, Ill.: Interstate Printers and Publishers, Inc., 1962.

———, *Voluntary Statewide Coordination in Public Higher Education.* Ann Arbor, Mich.: The University of Michigan, 1961.

College and University Business Administration. Washington, D.C.: American Council on Education, 1952 and 1955. 2 vols.

Committee on Government and Higher Education, *The Efficiency of Freedom.* Baltimore: Johns Hopkins Press, 1959.

Council of State Governments, *Higher Education in the Forty-Eight States.* Chicago: The Council, 1952.

Dodds, Harold W., *et al., Government Assistance to Universities in Great Britain.* New York: Columbia University Press, 1952.

Educational Policies Commission, *Higher Education in a Decade of Decision,* Chapter VII: "How Finance Higher Education." Washington, D.C.: National Education Association, 1957.

Glenny, Lyman A., *Autonomy of Public Colleges: The Challenge of Coordination.* New York: McGraw-Hill Book Company, Inc., 1959.

Harris, Seymour E., *Higher Education: Resources and Finance.* New York: McGraw-Hill Book Company, Inc., 1962.

Harris, Seymour E., (ed.), *Higher Education in the United States: The Economic Problems*. Cambridge, Mass.: Harvard University Press, 1960.

Hollis, Ernest V., *et al., Cost of Attending College*. U.S. Office of Education Bulletin No. 9. Washington, D.C.: USGPO, 1958.

Hungate, Thad L., *A New Basis of Support for Higher Education*. New York: Teachers College, Bureau of Publications, Columbia University, 1957.

Keezer, Dexter M., (ed.), *Financing Higher Education: 1960–70*. New York: McGraw-Hill Book Company, Inc., 1959.

Kidd, Charles V., *American Universities and Federal Research*. Cambridge, Mass.: Belknap Press of Harvard University Press, 1959.

McConnell, T. R., *A General Pattern for American Public Higher Education*. New York: McGraw-Hill Book Company, Inc., 1962.

Millett, John D., *Financing Higher Education in the United States*. Staff Report of the Commission on Financing Higher Education. New York: Columbia University Press, 1952.

Moos, Malcolm and Francis E. Rourke, *The Campus and the State*. Baltimore: Johns Hopkins Press, 1959.

Mushkin, Selma J., (ed.), *Economics of Higher Education*. U.S. Office of Education Bulletin No. 5. Washington, D.C.: USGPO, 1962.

Rich, Wilmer, *American Foundations and Their Fields,* 7th ed. New York: Raymond Rich Associates, 1955.

Rivlin, Alice M., *The Role of the Federal Government in Financing Higher Education*. Washington, D.C.: The Brookings Institution, 1961.

Russell, John Dale, *The Finance of Higher Education,* rev. ed. Chicago: University of Chicago Press, 1954.

Russell, John Dale and James I. Doi, *Manual for Studies of Space Utilization in Colleges and Universities*. Athens, Ohio: American Association of Collegiate Registrars and Admissions Officers, 1957.

Pollard, John A., *Fund-Raising for Higher Education*. New York: Harper & Row, Publishers, 1958.

President's Commission on Higher Education, *Higher Education for American Democracy,* Vol. V: *Financing Higher Education*. Washington, D.C.: USGPO, 1947.

President's Committee on Education Beyond the High School, *Second Report to the President,* Chapter IV: "Financing Higher Education." Washington, D.C.: The Committee, 1957.

Stewart, Ernest T., Jr., ed., *The "How To" of Educational Fund-Raising*. Washington, D.C.: American Alumni Council, 1956.

A Study of Income and Expenditures in Sixty Colleges—1953–54. Wellesley, Mass.: National Federation of College and University Business Officers Association, 1955.

The Sixty College Study: A Second Look—1957–58. Wellesley, Mass.: National Federation of College and University Business Officers Associations, 1960.

Vaizey, John, *The Economics of Education*. New York: The Crowell-Collier Publishing Co., 1962.

Index

A

Acceleration of college courses, 10, 11
Administration and general expense, 74, 75, 96
Advice to students and their families, 107-110
Agriculture, Department of, 54
Akron, Ohio, 34
Alaska, 52
Allen, H. K., 105
Allocated taxes, 40
Alumni giving, 24-26
American Association of University Professors, 15 n., 48
American Association of University Women, 48
American Council on Education, 13 n., 56
Anderson, William, 57
Appropriations by state legislatures, 40-42
Army Specialized Training Program, 8
Association of American Colleges, 82 n.
Association for Higher Education, 49
Association of State Universities and Land-Grant Colleges, 56
Athletics, intercollegiate, 71
Atomic Energy Commission, 54, 65
Auxiliary enterprises, 72-73
Axt, Richard G., 105

B

Background of financial support, 1-17
Bemis, Maynard, 12
Board of trustees, as a source of support, 26
British universities, 94
Brown University, 26
Buchanan, James, 51
Budget, federal, 12, 32
Budget, state executive system, 99-101
Budget, U.S. Bureau of the, 55
Business corporations, as donors, 21-22
Business cycle, the, 1, 3
Byse, Clark, 81 n., 82 n.

C

California, 27, 41, 96-98, 104
Carnegie, Andrew, 79
Carnegie Corporation of New York, 21
Carnegie Foundation for the Advancement of Teaching, 79
Charitable corporations, 29
Charitable trusts, 4, 21, 29, 30, 93
(*see also* Foundations, philanthropic)
Chicago, University of, 93
Church organizations, as sources of support, 23
Cincinnati, 34
Civilian Conservation Corps, 5
Cold war, the, 6, 11-13
College and University Business, 72
Colonial colleges, 38
Colorado, 44, 45, 104
Committee on Government and Higher Education, 46 n., 99 n.
Commonwealth Fund, 20
Community colleges, 17, 27, 35-37, 41, 69, 100
Conant, James Bryant, 107
Connolly, Raymond J., 9 n.
Conrad, Herbert S., 28 n.
Conscription, peacetime, 7-8
"Cooperative plan" of college education, 108
Coordination of statewide systems, 45-46, 86 n., 88
Cornell University, 37 n., 52
Cost of attending colleges, 107
Costs and income, trends affecting, 1-4
Council for Financial Aid to Education, 18, 20
Current expenditures, categories of, 71-83

D

Dartmouth College, 25, 38
Debt, national, interest on the, 12
Defense, Department of, 54
Depression of the 1930's, 5-7, 42, 107
Dodds, Harold W., 94 n.
Doi, James I., 74 n.
Dormitories and dining halls, 71

E

Economies in operation, dubious, 42
Education, U.S. Office of, 54, 57, 76
Educational and general expenditures, 73-75
Efficiency in higher education, 84-101
Eisenhower, Dwight D., 54
Eisenhower, Milton, 46 n.
Endowment funds, 29-30
 declining role of, 3-5
 investment of, 92-93
Endowment, "living," 4, 26
Enrollment trends, 13-17, 87-88
Estate and inheritance taxes, 4, 59
Exemptions from taxation, 39
Expenditures, categories of current, 71-83
Extension service, 37, 43, 74, 75

F

Faculty, excellence of, 90
Faculty salaries, 2, 4, 21, 25, 76-83
Farm Bureau, 36
Federal agencies, relationships with, 56-57
Federal Emergency Relief Administration, 5
Federal government support, 50-57
 Morrill Act, 51-52
 Depression and wartime measures, 52-53
 grants and contracts for research, 54-56
 grants and loans for plant construction, 53-54
 scholarships, fellowships, loans to students, 54
Federal Reserve Board, 3
Fees (*see* Student fees)
Fellowships, under federal programs, 54, 65-67, 108
Flint Junior College, 36-37
Florida, 39
Ford Foundation, 4, 21
Foreign aid, 12
Formulas for allocation of funds, 93-101
Fringe benefits, 78-80
Foundations, philanthropic, 4, 20-21

G

G.I. Bill, 53, 73
Gifts, current total of, 20
 restricted and unrestricted, defined, 19-20
Glenny, Lyman A., 45 n.
Guggenheim Foundation, 21

H

Hanson, Judge, 81
Harris, Seymour E., 15, 59, 60, 108
Harvard College, 38
Harvard Law Review, 81 n.
Harvard University, 19, 59, 108
Hatch Act of 1887, 52
Hawaii, 52
Hayden Foundation, 21
Health, Education, and Welfare, Department of, 57
Henry, David D., 85, 86
Herge, H. C., 9 n.
Hollis, Ernest V., 28 n.
Hungate, Thad L., 104

I

Illinois, 50
Income, *per capita,* 104
Income, sources of, 18-57
 from non-tax sources, 18-30
 from tax sources, 31-57
Income tax rates, 4, 6
Indiana, 44, 45, 50
Industrial productivity, 103
Inflation, effects of, 3
Instruction, costs of, 85-90
Instruction, excellence of, 89
International comparisons, 105
Investments, management of, 92
 (*see also* Endowment funds)
Interest rates, fluctuations, 2
Iowa, 44
Issues regarding the sources of support, 58-70

J

Johns Hopkins University, 39
Joughin, Louis, 82 n.
Junior colleges (*see* Community colleges)

K

Kansas, 34, 44
Kellogg Foundation, 21
Kentucky, 34, 95, 98
Kidd, Charles V., 55 n.
Korean G.I. Bill, 53, 73

L

Land-grant colleges, 37-38, 43-44, 51-52
Lawrence College, 26
Leaves, sabbatical, 79-80
Library expense, 74-76, 89, 95
Lilly Endowment, 21
Lincoln, Abraham, 51
Loans and grants for college building, 6, 53-54
Loans for students (*see* Student loans)
Lobbying, 46-49
Local community sources of support, 23-24, 33-37
Louisiana, 40, 104
Ludlum, Robert P., 2 n.

M

McConnell, T. R., 45 n.
Management of investments, 92
Maryland, 39
Massachusetts, 38
Massachusetts Institute of Technology, 52
Massachusetts, University of, 52
Mellon Fund, 21
Miami University (Ohio), 50
Miami, University of (Florida), 39
Michigan, 44, 45, 50, 51, 104
Millage taxes, 40
Millett, John D., 3, 4 n.
Minnesota, University of, 57
Montana, 104
Moos, Malcolm, 46 n.
Morrill Act, 51-52
Morrill, Justin S., 51
Municipal universities, 34
Murphy, Franklin D., 105 n.

N

Naftalin, Arthur, 98-99
National Aeronautics and Space Administration, 54, 65 n.
National Defense Education Act, 57, 65-69, 73, 109
National Education Association, 15, 48, 49, 76
National Institutes of Health, 54, 65
National policy, higher education as an instrument of, 16, 69
National Federation of College and University Business Officers' Associations, 75 n.
National Science Foundation, 54, 55, 56, 65, 73
National Youth Administration, 5, 52, 73
Navy V-12 Program, 8
Nebraska, 34
New Hampshire, 38
New Jersey, 22, 39
New York, 33, 34, 37 n., 64, 65 n.
New York City, 34, 64
Non-academic personnel, 83
North Central Association of Colleges and Secondary Schools, 89
North Central Association Quarterly, 86 n.
Nuffield College, 94

O

Occupations, upgrading of, 14-15
Office of Education, U.S., 54, 57, 76
Officer Candidate Schools, 8-9
Ohio, 34, 45, 50, 51, 105
Ohio State University, 37, 42
Ohio University, 50
Oklahoma, 45, 95-96, 98
Old Age and Survivors' Insurance, 78
Oregon, 43-44
Ostar, Allan W., 61 n.
"Overhead" costs of sponsored research, 55
Oxford University, 94

P

Parent-teacher associations, 48
Pearl Harbor, 7
Pennsylvania, 38, 51, 104
People's Republic of China, 13
Philanthropic foundations, 4, 20-21
Pittsburgh, University of, 38, 63
Plant construction, federal grants and loans for, 53-54
Plant operation and maintenance, 85
Plant utilization, 91-92
Population trends, 13-15
Post-war period, the, 10-14
Pressey, Sidney L., 10
Price curve, the, 2, 11
Princeton University, 3 n., 22
Private donors, 19-26
Private philanthropy, the future of, 59-60
Proprietary institutions, 27
Protestant denominations, as sources of support, 23

Public funds, support from, 16-17, 31-57
Public lands, federal grants of, 50-52
Public relations, 36-37, 46-50
Public Works Administration, 6, 53
Puerto Rico, 52

Q

Queens College, 102

R

Reconstruction Finance Corporation, 6, 53
Reeves, Floyd W., 89 n.
Research, "departmental," 73, 75, 76
Research, federal grants and contracts for, 54-56
Research, "organized," 73-74
Reserve Officers' Training Corps, 9
Retirement systems, 79
Revenue system, the, 12, 32-33
Rockefeller Foundation, 21
Roman Catholic institutions, 23
Rourke, Francis E., 46 n.
Russell, John Dale, 89 n.

S

Sabbatical leaves, 79-80
"Sacred cows," 92
"Scholar incentive program," 64-65
Scholarships, 54, 64-65, 108
Selective Service System, 7, 56
Sixty College Study, the, 75
Sloan Foundation, 21
Smith-Lever Act, 52
Social security, 6, 78-79
South Dakota, 80-81
South Dakota State College, 80
Southern Association of Colleges and Secondary Schools, 95
State executive budget system, 99-100
State federations of women's clubs, 48
State legislature, the province of the, 99-101
State subsidies to community colleges, 41
State support, 38-49
  of community colleges, 41
  of private institutions, 38-39
  of public institutions, 40-41
  of state institutions, 42-46
State systems of taxation, 30-33, 39
  (*see also* Taxes)
State Universities Association, 56, 61 n.
States, comparisons among, 104
Stoke, Harold W., 69, 102
Student aids, 64-68, 72, 108
  as a category of expenditure, 72
  the rationale of, 64-68
  (*see also* Fellowships; Scholarships)
Student fees, 16, 27-28, 34, 60-63, 105-108
Student loans, 67-69, 71, 108-109
Students' Army Training Corps, 7
Students, out-of-state, 103-104
Sumner, William Graham, 25
Surplus materials, federal gifts of, 54

T

Taft, Senator Robert A., 11
Tax collections, federal, state, and local, 12
Taxes, 32-35
  exemptions from, 39
  by local subdivisions, 33-35
  state income, 33
  state and local property, 33
  state sales, 32-33
Tax funds as a source of income, 31-57
Teacher-student ratio, 90-91
Teachers' Insurance and Annuity Association, 79
Television, closed circuit, 91
Temple University, 38
Tenure, for faculty members, 80-83
Texas, 61, 96, 98
Texas, University of, 51
Toledo, 34
Trend toward public support, the, 69-70
Trends affecting costs and income, 1-17
Trytten, M. H., 8 n.
Tuition, (*see* Student fees)
Twentieth Century Fund, 21

U

Union of Socialist Soviet Republics, 12, 13, 63, 105-106
Unit costs of instruction, 85-90
Utah, 44
Utilization of plant facilities, 91-92
U.S. Census Bureau, 13
U.S. Public Health Service, 13

V

Veterans, as students, 14, 53-54

W

Wages of non-academic employees, 76
Washington (State of), 44
Waste, sources of, 102-107
Wesleyan University, 25
Where the money comes from, 18-57
Where the money goes, 71-83
Wisconsin, 39, 50
Women students, 62-64, 68
"Work-study" plan, 108
World War I, 7, 8, 39
World War II, 5, 7-10, 73, 77
Worzella Case, 81
Wriston, Henry M., 26

Y

Yale University, 19, 25